# Missing in Paris

## Hope and Resilience

By Dave Smith

This book is a work of Non Fiction and the stories contained herein are true or based on true facts to the best of the authors knowledge. No part of this book is to be copied or reproduced in any form, by written, electronic or mechanical, including photocopying, recording, or by any information retrieval system without the permission in writing from the publishing company.

The right of Dave Smith to be identified as author of this work has been asserted by him in accordance with Copyright, Designs, and Patents Act, 1988

Although every precaution has been taken in the preparation of this book, the publishers and author assume no responsibility for errors or omissions. Neither is any liability assumed for damages resulting from the use of the information contained within this book. While the book contains QR and webpage links to other websites and resources we do not claim any connection with them. They are provided for your own use for the purpose of research and knowledge. Nor can we give credence to these sites, they are there for you to make your own informed decisions.

The copyright remains with the perspective copyright holders. Images are used purely for editorial use and to help find other missing children and adults.

Published by Three Zombie Dogs® Ltd Publishing at McLaughlin's Close, Derry. All rights reserved. Copyright ©2020 and by any other respective copyright holders. ISBN: 9781912039098.

Printing of this book is done by Ingram, Amazon and other worldwide licenced and authorised distributors or printers. Printers must adhere to sustainability and have "Green Polices" in place. The publisher is part of plant a tree programs to offset the printing of every book.

A copy of this book has been deposited at the Legal Deposit including the Irish, Scottish, Welsh and British Libraries.

If you come across any broken QR code links in this book, please let the publisher know at: missingQR@missinginparis.com if a person is found and you would like their photograph removed from this book then contact missing@missinginparis.com and they will be removed and a new release of the book will be issued. We respect your privacy at all times.

Book Cover design by Olivia Pro Design

Front Cover photograph (Sacré-Coeur): Dave Smith

Back Cover photograph (Photograph contains actors): Verkoka

# For
# Alicia

# Contents

| | |
|---|---|
| Introduction | P 12 |
| In the wrong place at the right time | P 17 |
| Character names used within this book | P 19 |

## Missing In Paris – The Search — Page 20

| | |
|---|---|
| Mario, or reliving and telling his story | P 137 |

## Resources and Further Reading

| | |
|---|---|
| Authors words | P 138 |
| Missing Teenagers in France | P 140 |
| A few minutes of your time is all the Missing ask. | P 141 |
| Every parent's worst nightmare | P 144 |
| Hope Poem and Breathing Exercise | P 145 |
| MissingInParis.com | P 146 |
| Missing: Leah Croucher Age 19 | P 147 |
| Hearing voices, you are not alone | P 149 |
| The voices in my head, Eleanor Langdon | P 154 |
| Hearing voices an Insiders-Guide | P 155 |
| What the voices inside my head say | P 156 |
| Hearing voices, Juno's story | P 157 |
| Lost in reality hearing voices | P 158 |
| Hearing Voices Network | P 159 |
| Coping Strategies for hearing voices | P 162 |
| Manchester NHS | P 163 |

| | |
|---|---|
| Psychosis research | P 164 |
| The God Dilemma | P 165 |
| Mental health issues | P 168 |
| Ruby Wax on mindfulness | P 171 |
| The one gift Santa couldn't deliver | P 172 |
| Humanity in Action | P 173 |
| The right of an adult to disappear | P 174 |
| Exploited | P 176 |
| What you can do when a person goes missing | P 178 |
| A story of Hope | P 181 |
| Adverse Childhood Experiences (ACE's) | P 182 |
| Northern Ireland ACE animation | P 192 |
| Teen brain development | P 193 |
| Brain hand model | P 194 |
| ACE Questionnaire Missing in Paris adaptation | P 196 |
| The education system | P 203 |
| What is school for by Prince EA | P 215 |
| School Principal reacts to Prince EA | P 216 |
| Tragic news re school and religion | P 217 |
| Divorce/Marriage | P 221 |
| Abortion | P 223 |
| The main purpose of Sex | P 226 |
| The only true Bastards | P 227 |
| How relationships shape us | P 230 |
| Drugs | P 231 |

| | |
|---|---|
| Adversity | P 235 |
| Suicide Awareness and help | P 236 |
| Missingpeople.org.uk | P 237 |
| Missing in Paris Link | P 238 |
| Good news from the newspapers | P 240 |
| Support contact details in France | P 242 |
| Do you have a website | P 243 |
| Madeline McCann | P 244 |
| Resilience | P 246 |
| 3 Points to remember | P 285 |
| Quotations of Resilience | P 286 |
| Quotations of Hope | P 290 |
| Missing Persons Poem | P 291 |
| Authors Pillar & 3 Causes | P 292 |
| About the Author | P 294 |
| SMARITANS and GLOBAL Helplines | P 300 |

You will have to download a QR app if you want to use the interactive parts of the book. Please note, we do not place any form of advertising within our QR codes.

Some of the contents in this book can be mentally challenging and may open old wounds. We recommend talking with someone if your adversities overwhelm you. Don't not suffer alone, you are loved. There are global helplines on the last page of this book

**SMARITANS UK Helpline - 24/7, - Telephone: 116 123**

# Dedicated to

...the tens of thousands of missing and abducted children and Adults around the world

# And may the

... Governments of the world be bombarded by requests to pump money into the destruction of the Paedophile and human trafficking networks that currently exist.

# And may they

... Actually do something constructive about solving this problem and obliterating this one hundred and fifty billion dollar criminalised industry... Today rather than Tomorrow.

# One child or adult missing, abducted or trafficked

# Is ONE to many!

# 25th of May

## Is

# International Missing Children's day

https://www.icmec.org/global-missing-childrens-center/imcd/

# 10th of September

Is

# International Suicide Prevention Day

https://www.iasp.info/wspd2019/

# 10th of October

Is

# International Mental Health Day

https://www.mentalhealth.org.uk/campaigns/world-mental-health-day

# Introduction by the Author

This story is based on Mario's recall of events that occurred in 2018 when he was searching for a missing teenager in Paris. Some information and character names have been changed to protect the privacy of the people involved.

When a person goes missing families want everyone on earth to know that their child or family member is missing and they desperately ask for your help.

However, when the missing are found the families want privacy so that they can rebuild their fragile lives. It's not that they are not thankful, they are more than grateful to everyone that has helped. While research has demonstrated that it is better for a person's mental health if they can talk openly and freely about what has happened to them, some are not ready to commence that leap.

One day perhaps Alicia will be in a position to share her own personal story, thereby assisting others in a similar, unfortunate and traumatised position to begin their healing journey.

This book only touches on the trauma that Alicia and her family faced and endured on her disappearance from her home in Barcelona. A family traumatised want only one thing, they want their child (regardless of age) back safe and sound.

This story is the journey of "Mario the Searcher" and the search for the missing teenager. Mario said, "it was similar to searching for 'a needle in a haystack', it was engulfed in many facets of understanding oneself, and embracing the journeys trials and tribulations while attempting to care for one's own mental health."

You will experience Mario's journey in the search for Alicia. He experienced many emotions including; joy, sorrow and physical pain. At times he felt a sense of uselessness stretching from the deepest depths of depression to a near mental breakdown with suicidal thoughts.

I would like to make it clear that the research section is not part of Mario's story nor is the author suggesting that any of the research information has been experienced by the characters in the story. The research section is part of the author's roadmap and self-help books designed towards helping people with mental health issues.

Therefore, the research section represents the authors viewpoints, obtained via education, experience and research. Over the last four years I have been involved in ACE's (Adverse Childhood Experiences) research and obtained a diploma in 2019. I'm part of the campaign to raise awareness of ACE's and how society needs to embrace and develop new ways of helping children and adults through their adversities.

In the research section of the book there are interviews with people who have endured adversity in their lives and they want to impart that information to help others in a similar situation. But every person is different and it can take longer for some to recover or indeed to be able to talk about what happened to them. The past cannot be changed, but your future mental health can learn and heal from events in the past. Each person has the ability to reshape what has happened to them and to forge a brighter future via resilience.

This book is further dedicated to those that find themselves in a similar position to Alicia. Attempting to find a missing person can lead you to depths of despair and depression that you can only imagine in your nightmares. So spare a thought for the thousands of children and adults still missing. And remember there is always hope, hope is the cornerstone of support that will provide you with the resilience to keep going.

Please read the resources presented in this book with an open mind, and it may just assist you in taking care of yourself and your family's mental health. Nothing in your earthly existence is more important than the health, equality and freedom of every person on earth.

In a world of many faiths, religious beliefs and non-religious beliefs, some people may believe that the journey of this story is an act of GOD. However, I ask you one question,

Who's GOD?

This book is not intended in any way to represent a particular religion, faith or belief. Mario is what you would call a holistic believer in the 'Future, Present and Past as ONE' and would be considered an atheist to the current mainstream religious believes. However, others within Mario's family believed that it was their Christian faith that assisted in the search for Alicia. As Mario said, that indeed is a story for another book.

**The 10th of October each year is national mental health awareness day. Moreover, why wait for this one particular day, please take the time to 'Talk and Listen' to someone at any time… on any day… in any week… You never know, you may have just saved someone's life.** ☺

They say that you should never talk about religion, politics, education, drugs, sex and a few other things. And since this book is also about self-help mental health, and these topics are indeed part of everyone's current existence, I will talk about them as they can have a drastic effect on a person's mental health.

While my beliefs might not be shared by everyone that reads this book, I make no excuse for bringing these subjects into the public arena to necessitate a change in the current fabric of our society and existence. These topics are most definitely some of the conductors that shape the mental health for everyone including children and adults that go missing.

I would like to point out that I know many good and great people within education and religion. Therefore, my comments within this book do not condemn everyone within these organisations. There are always a few bad apples in every basket but that does not imply the whole basket of apples are bad.

However, there comes a time when a closer look is required and a 'fix' where necessary. First and foremost, freedom, freedom from harm, true & pure equality, and individual rights all come first before anything else. The missing, the abused, the trafficked and the abducted have all been denied those basic of rights.

Each person in society can make a difference in helping to find a missing person. This book will demonstrate how with little effort you can make a difference in finding a missing person.

This book will help you understand mental health issues and come to the conclusion that there is nothing to be ashamed of. Mental health issues are no different from any other health issue you may have. Your brain is no different from other injuries, sickness or disease that your body has.

Mental health matters, and mental health deserve and needs the same care and assistance as you would expect from any other aliment that you might be treated for.

# In the wrong place at the right time

I recall a story that was told to me: Johnny a mental health worker was driving along a bridge that was known for people jumping to the waters below and ultimately to their deaths. A young man who was suffering from severe recurring depression and normally would not have been in this part of town, was standing looking downwards towards the fast running river with its many undercurrents. This was a bridge know for many suicide attempts, the majority of which were fatal.

He was known to Johnny via his work as a social worker, hence why Johnny knew instantly that there was a problem. He stopped his car, got out and approached the young man:

"Hi Bill, how are you?"...

"I don't know, I feel lonely and a bit low today"...

Johnny touched Bills shoulder and said, "come with me and I'll give you lift home and we can chat in the car"....

"I think I'll just stay here mucker" came the reply.

Bill said with a tone of concern, "If I leave you here and something happens then I will be questioned by my superiors to why I left you alone and then I will be in bother, do you want that to happen to me?"...

Bill replied, "No... ok I'll come with you, mucker"

Was this an act of coincidence or...? Neither Johnny nor Bill should have been anywhere near that bridge on that day, yet they both found themselves together at that exact moment in time.

However, it should be reasonable for you to ask a simple question if you see someone acting a bit out of the ordinary, especially at a site know for suicide attempts. You could stop and ask, "Are you Ok... would you like to talk?"

And if you are in any doubt on the response you receive, seek further assistance by phoning the police or any other appropriate emergency service.

This book will give you an insight in how to plan and begin looking for a missing person while looking after your own mental health. While Mario discarded his own health he admits that without your own good mental health you certainly will not be able to effectively help find the missing in a constructive manner. Your wellbeing and mental health are important if you are to productively continue searching for a missing person. As such you need some form of resilience to keep you going.

# Character names used within the book

The story is written by the author after holding interviews with Mario. The story is told from the viewpoint of Mario who is searching for Alicia. The names of the people involved have been changed to respect their privacy. This is an account from the eyes of Mario and represents his viewpoints of what he experienced while searching for Alicia in Paris.

**Alicia:** The Missing Teenager

**Sofia:** The searchers Partner

**Laura:** Alicia's Mum

**Antonio:** Alicia's Stepdad

**Alma:** Alicia's Sister

**Luis:** Alicia's Dad

**Father Andre:** One of the Priests

**Aurnia:** A woman who helped

**Ethan:** The Teenager from Norway

**Mario:** The Searcher

# The Search
# Missing in Paris

It was the end of spring 2018, it wasn't the mild and cool weather as normally expected for Barcelona for this time of the year. The temperatures soared to that of a hot summer's day, and we headed for the beach.

My son and his friend were following jelly fish while swimming in the sea. I sat near the edge of the water sifting hot sand through my fingers while watching my children play. They swam around the jellyfish, while shouting, "Do these sting?" I shrugged my shoulders and shouted, "You will soon find out." I looked over to my left and thought I recognised two young women and a child playing near me. It turned out to be Alicia and her sister.

I hadn't seen Alicia for quite some time, probably at least two years or so. Alicia told me about her studies at university and how she might take a year out before beginning again, and perhaps her partying played a bigger role than her studies. Her story brought back memories of when I was at University. Indeed many teenagers have experienced the same freedom rituals, a rite of passage to becoming independent and settling down to the university way of life.

We chatted for a while, but I could sense that she was not entirely happy, it's difficult to explain but I felt she was in another place and she appeared slightly troubled. I thought at the time her education was on her mind and that possibly she was unsure what she wanted to do in life, as all teenagers do. Adulthood can be a challenging time. I told Alicia if she ever needed to talk she was always welcome to come and talk with Sofia and me. Little did I know what was drastically about to happen in the coming months?

## Day 1: The Phone Call
### Friday 21st September 2018

Sofia's phone rang, she answered it and continued to walk around the room, nodding her head in acknowledgment of what was being said. I could see the blood drain from her face. Soon a sense of loss became the birth of her crumbling body towards the slouch of despair as she sat down on the sofa.

With tears in her eyes she put her hands to the side of her face. Sofia then said, "Alicia has gone missing."

You hear about missing children and teenagers quite regularly but you never think that it will be one from your family, do you?

At this stage they had no idea what had happened to Alicia, and what was the reasoning behind her disappearance?

Later, a further phone call outlined that Alicia was indeed missing. Missing of her own accord.

[Moreover, when a person goes missing without notifying a friend or family member then the initial assumption should always be that something unfamiliar is at play. It definitely should not be considered routine for a person just to disappear without any prior warning regardless of their age or the authority's interpretation of who can be a possible missing person.

Such drastic actions can point to a mental health concern or relationship, family or health problem. Sometimes a person just needs to get up and leave, but usually not without either pre warning a friend or calling within a few hours to let others know that they are safe and well. This should be the ultimate proof to the authorities that help is urgently needed, and with this in mind search and rescue can be validated quicker and more efficiently regardless of a person's age. Thus resulting in a far greater chance of finding the missing person.]

Alicia's stepdad managed to trace her movements from leaving her house via a door CCTV camera. The camera footage showed Alicia entering a taxi that she had ordered via her mobile phone. The taxi company confirmed that they took her to a bus that was destined for the airport. The police in their initial investigation discovered that she had boarded a plane from El Prat de Llobregat Aeropuerto to Paris.

But why Paris?

Her parents thought that perhaps Alicia was going to Lourdes as she became somewhat religious in the last few months...Talking about GOD in a manner that would certainly reflect an unhealthy relationship between present reality and her faith as a Christian.

It was also suggested that she went to the airport with the view to take the first available flight, and it just happened to be Paris.

When I spoke to Alicia at the beach, she made no references to religion or God, however she did say that she would like to do some travelling.

# Day 2: Considered an Adult
## Saturday 22ⁿᵈ September 2018

Frustration began to make a home for its self within the family. At nineteen years of age Alicia was considered an adult. This teenager missing in Paris was almost lost in the eyes of the legal system. In the eyes of the law an adult can declare themselves to be missing and not to be found.

Alicia's parents tried to uncover details of her bank spending to attempt to track her down. The bank were unable to provide such information due to data protection laws'. Likewise the police were not in a position to provide information as she was an adult, an adult that deserves privacy. But in the eyes of the family this privacy was nonsense and a matter of extreme concern and worry.

To further fuel the situation, everyone was unsure of her mental state. If indeed she had a mental health problem then the motion towards search and rescue would have increased dramatically.

However, that was not the case, and the wheel of action ground forward slower than what it should have been. During this time her family attempted to persuade the authorities with the help of their municipality Politian. They tried to prove and provide evidence that Alicia did have mental health issues and could be at risk in order to expedite the search.

As I pointed out earlier, a change in the law for an assumed missing adult is absolutely required as a matter of urgency. When the authorities don't search for a missing adult, it assists the perpetrators to commit acts of abuse, murder and trafficking of the missing. Especially those defined as an adult, 18 years of age and upwards. Petition your local Politian's for a change to the definition in law of a missing adult. The missing deserve to be found. Would you want your 18, 19, 20+ daughter or son to have fewer search rights because of being defined as an adult?

If an adult goes missing without leaving proof that they are in sane mind then they should be searched for immediately.

Alicia's parents were busy trying to get information from her friends and from her computer left behind. Friends either did not know anything or they had become uncooperative as friends do when they think that they are protecting someone and do not really grasp the nature of the actual emergency.

Alicia's phone was dead with no signal at all, any police trace would have been useless. It was quite possible that Alicia sold her iPhone to help pay her way in a new country or indeed it could have been lost or stolen.

Alicia had limited financial resources but a few days before disappearing she had visited her dad and had asked him for £500. He put the money directly into her bank, unaware of what she was about to do.

The family asked the bank manager to trace any withdrawals from her account, but they encountered a brick wall. Data protection and the fact that she was an adult stopped the bank from assisting in a timely manner. The family had to convince the police to investigate her bank account, and again bureaucracy digs its claws in.

The most important tactic in any missing person's recovery is in the speed that search and rescue is carried out. The chance of finding the person reduces drastically as time passes. The "golden hour" did not apply in this case, but still every hour would be equally precious. A change to the law, legal and political system to become that of an understanding of time being an essential factor in the recovery of a missing child, teenager or adult. I can't overstate the need for this change in the law.

Moreover, if a missing person is "suspected" to have mental health issues. Then this "suspected" missing person should indeed be a matter of immediate concern and instant access to any official records by family and police investigators should be mandatory.

# Adult Disappearance Law in France

An adult can go off without letting anyone know or sever links with his family (unlike children who are subject to parental authority). Given an individual's right of freedom, no one can oblige them to get back in contact with their family. If a person goes off voluntarily and there is nothing suspicious about their disappearance, you need to undertake a "recherche dans l'intérêt des familles" (RIF) [search on behalf of the family]. This procedure can take several months.

The Recherche dans l'intérêt des familles (RIF) procedure

1. Go to the Préfecture, but the RIF can also be registered at Police stations or Gendarmeries.
2. Provide an official document proving the link between the requester and the missing person.
3. Once found, the adult is informed that his family is looking for him but his contact details can only be passed on with his permission.
4. If he refuses, the person who initiated the RIF is informed that the adult has been located but does not wish to get back in contact.

If, despite the initial voluntary nature of the departure, the disappearance appears worrying to you, You can write to the local Procureur de la République du tribunal de grande instance [Public prosecutor at the equivalent of the county court]. The letter (sent signed-for and registered) is to convince the Prosecutor to launch a worrying disappearance enquiry. The resources given to this will be greater than a normal search on behalf of the family.

## Day 3: Frustration
## Sunday 23rd September 2018

The search for information continues and frustration for the family leads to a state of extreme worry and anxiety. The authorities work more efficiently as they now believe that maybe Alicia has a mental health issue. Talks are being held between the French and Spanish Police forces.

Alicia's disappearance has been reported in the local and International newspapers. Social media is being used to try and get others involved in the search for her, especially in Paris and Lourdes.

The family used social media to send out missing alerts and friends and colleagues from Mario's work circulated Alicia's photo to organisations in France. Mario made missing posters and they were distributed by email to various social media sites in France. A missing person's email account was created to handle sightings that were derived from the posters. However, we never received any sightings apart from the odd good luck message.

The police have now located Alicia via her bank transactions and found her at a hostel in Paris city centre.

Their daughter had been found and she was safe. They were anxious but at last their faith had born fruit. While the family attempted to make sense of this nightmare and ordeal, a sense of hope and relief eased Laura and Antonio's negative emotions. Soon they would be at the side of their daughter and all would be well again. [Looking after your own mental health in these circumstances is easier said than done. But none the less your mental health is paramount if you are to survive and to find your loved one.]

The French police escorted Alicia's parents to the place she was staying, Alicia was questioned by the police with her parents present. She gave the impression and came forward as a normal nineteen year old. Alicia was a typical teenager who just wanted to travel on her own without any interference from anyone.

Alicia apologised to her parents and the police for her abrupt and unannounced departure from her home. Alicia explained that she felt the need to leave and travel and enjoy her young life and did not think of letting anyone know.

However, I firmly believe that when a person takes off without any pre warning then this highlights that indeed something is wrong, a part of their life is crying for help but does not know how to ask for it. These overwhelming internal emotions take hold and begin to form an unhealthy relationship between mind and reality.

[While Alicia lived with her parents, for others that live on their own it could have been weeks or longer before anyone knew that they were missing.]

After the meeting, Alicia reluctantly hugged her parent's goodbye, but agreed to meet them in the morning at her hostel to talk further. Again this lack of empathy, and a pattern out with her normal behaviour was a sign that Alicia was not her jolly usual self.

Newspapers and social media now reported Alicia as 'found, safe and well.' As a result the search for Alicia ceased and the French and Spanish police stopped all current investigations. And all social media postings were stopped and Alicia was reported as found.

The family were now in a situation of bewilderment. For the days before Alicia was found they lived in an unknown domain of anxiety, sadness, sleepless nights and constant adrenalin that kept them going for their daughters search. Now, that Alicia had been found their body begins to return to a normal state. But your body cannot do that immediately, it takes time for those feelings to settle down. And these feelings can take you on a journey of questions.

A lack of understanding begins to take hold, "but why did she not say when and where she was going and for how long? " Again I repeat myself, these are signs that something is not quite right. But how do you actually get your child to open up so that you can be their rock of safety? In Laura and Antonio's case, they did not get that time for questions and answers as Alicia had made her mind up and was gone without telling anyone.

While Alicia had her reasons for travelling to Paris her parents had their reasons of concern for Alicia's safety. When a child becomes an adult in the eyes of the law and that adult decides to leave and go unannounced to somewhere in the world, what rights do a concerned parent have?

## Day 4: No forwarding address
## Monday 24th of September 2018

As arranged the night before, Alicia's parents made their way from their hotel to the hostel, which was literally around the corner. However, Alicia had checked out and was nowhere to be seen, nor did she leave a forwarding address. She left a bag of spare clothes that her mum had given her the night before, with a note… "Please give these clothes to charity."

Put yourself in the parent's shoes: You found your daughter after several days of worry, anxiety, and possibly nightmares where you imagined all the worst case scenarios.

You finally get to see and talk with your daughter in a foreign country. Then you lose her again. Only this time there are no authorities willing to help. Why would they become involved again when Alicia was interviewed by the police with the parents at that meeting, and she was found to be in a normal teenager state of mind?

Can you imagine the frustration of being in a foreign country and the tremendous barriers to impede any new search and by yourself? Do you leave Alicia alone in Paris and go back to Spain to await for her to contact you? After all she did convince her parents and the authorities that she was well and ok.

I can feel the pain of this dilemma, can you imagine being in this situation?

**What would you do?**

## Day 5: Without assistance
## Tuesday 25<sup>th</sup> of September 2019

Alicia's mum and stepdad continue to search around Paris for Alicia. But this time without any assistance from the Spanish or French authorities.

They were now fully alone in their quest to find their daughter in a country that was foreign to them nor did they speak French.

They had leads from notes left in her room. These pointed to a priest just outside Paris and talks with Father Andre commenced.

It transpired that Alicia had asked the priest to help with accommodation and for finding work with the nuns on her arrival in Paris.

Father Andre unable to help Alicia told her that she should come back to speak with him in a few days' time and to attend his mass on Friday.

But Alicia never went back.

# The Searcher and Search
## 25th September 2018

Since Alicia went missing, I knew that time was of the essence. I had offered myself to help find Alicia since day one of her going missing. I believed in my heart that I could find her. It's difficult to explain, but I had an overwhelming feeling that was pulling me towards the perception that I could help find Alicia. I had signs already registering in my thoughts and had dreams that were pulling me to Paris.

But instead I remained at work, creating missing posters, updating social media locally and in Paris. However my mind was continually telling me to go to Paris and help with the search. Many times I suggested to Sofia who was Alicia's Aunt and said, "I can help and that I should go to Paris." That's how overwhelming my feelings were. Plus I had old acquaintances in France that might be able to lend a hand with the search.

Later that morning I got a call at work, Sofia said that Laura would like me to go to Paris and help search for Alicia.

# The Journey to Paris
## 25th September 2018

I booked an online EasyJet direct flight to Paris, however it was going to be a tight timeframe to catch the flight. I left work immediately after my flight was booked, returned home to collect my bag that Sofia had packed for me and my passport and left for the airport.

I was about to travel and commence a search in a city with a population of 2.14 million and with over 70 million visitors each year. It is claimed that Paris is one of the most densely populated cities in the world, and is a city with many cultures and diversities. The pure scale and vastness of Paris was overwhelming, I had set myself up from the start with hope. But any possible failure would have an impact on my own and my family's mental health.

I was so sure that I would find Alicia, anything less would have been mental disaster for me. Furthermore, I believed that not being born from the family would allow Alicia to speak freely with me. And I could help Alicia get what she wanted, like making sure she did not have to sleep on the street or go without food, basically ensuring she had a healthy structure in place. While my heart knew that there was a possible problem with Alicia's outlook on life, I held onto the hope that she was only a typical teenager looking to spread her wings.

My primary goal was to find Alicia and if she wanted to stay in Paris then put in place an infrastructure where she would be safe. And indeed one that her family could be secure in the knowledge that Alicia was safe and contactable.

Without knowing where Alicia was, toxic stress became the daily experience for her parents. Day in and day out, not knowing where she was, did she have a place to stay, was Alicia safe? Can you imagine not knowing where your daughter is? And that you could not contact her to check all was ok. This situation was a breeding ground for abductors, sexual predators and traffickers. Not knowing your Childs location is a state of mind where no one wants to be.

The traffic and roadworks were torture and finally I arrived at the airport, but missed the EasyJet direct flight to Paris by a few minutes. I decided there was no way I was waiting until tomorrow, so I got out my laptop and searched for other flights. EasyJet tried to assist me, but they were limited to their own flights.

I found a flight to Stanstead and then a connecting flight from Stanstead to Paris that same night. I arrived in Paris late in the evening of Tuesday 25$^{th}$ September 2018 with HOPE filling my heart.

Even today I can visually recall the moment I arrived at Charles de Gaul airport. I arrived with a sense of hope that I was going to find Alicia and it was going to be tonight. However, when I walked down the corridors past passport control the immensity of Paris even in the darkness of the night overcame me, and my hope turned to despair. Not despair for myself but despair that I may have built up the hope of Alicia's family and here I am now looking for a 'needle in a haystack'.

This hopelessness was short lived and I regained my strength and hope. Hope gave me the positive encouragement to continue with my plan of action. Without hope, I was of no use and would have been better off staying at home.

My plan was to create achievable goals with my overall goal of finding Alicia.

I recall this goal quotation by Lawrence Peter who was a Canadian Educator, *"If you don't know where you are going, you will probably end up somewhere else."* So it was imperative that I had a clear vision of where I was going with my goals.

I believed I had the qualities to effectively search for a missing person, my background within project management should assist me with the strategic design of my overall "search and find" plan. Plus persistence was my stamina and my middle name. However, what I totally forgot about was the personal and emotional side of searching for a missing person, especially when it is a person from your own family.

This emotional side would certainly bring a new meaning and aspect to my search.

*"It doesn't make you weak to ask for help."* Billie Eilish on mental health.

# First Night in Paris
## 25th and 26th September 2018

My first task was to find a place to stay for the night. So I began to rule out hotels and turned to hostels that provided accommodation in the monetary range that Alicia might be able to afford.

I checked in at my hostel around 11 pm, and showed the receptionist a photo of Alicia, but they had not seen her. Probably wishful thinking on my part. The hostel that I had picked came from a sign that I had.

After I placed my one bag in my shared room, I went outside and walked around the streets, checked out some bars were teenagers might hang out. I got back to my hostel around 3 am and planned my next day's goals, getting to sleep around 4 am.

I arose at 7am, had breakfast consisting of orange juice and bread with jam. I showed the guests at the hostel a poster of Alicia and asked if they had seen her, but again no positive result.

Due to the religious nature of Alicia's behaviour before going missing, I decided to concentrate my search efforts on

- (A) Locating churches and finding out their mass times. I spoke to priests and their ministries, I also left photographs and my contact details.
- (B) Visiting hostels and leaving missing posters
- (C) Walking around the streets when going from chapel to hostel, hoping to see her.
- (D) Sometimes using the underground at night to move from one area to another in case Alicia was resting on the subways.
- (E) Visiting Bars and Clubs at night, especially pubs that the young ones frequented.
- (F) Visiting the river embankments that young people would hang around to drink and smoke weed.
- (G) Checking homeless shelters
- (H) Phoning hospitals for admissions

I met up with Laura and Antonio later that morning and had a coffee in an Irish bar in the Moulin Rouge district. They filled me in on what had occurred since they arrived. They both looked stressed to the hilt and that was an understatement.

It was now time for them both to leave and catch the bus to the airport and head back home. Though they were extremely frustrated and sad, they still held on to the belief that Alicia was ok. However I do think that deep down they knew something was not quite right with Alicia's emotions.

We gave each other a hug and we cried. It was difficult for them to leave Paris without their daughter. Laura and Antonio went home to try and muster some assistance from their local authorities. Only this time it would be harder to muster any enthusiasm for a new search after the French police report.

It is unimaginable to know that your daughter is missing in a foreign city and that you have no way of contacting her. The frustration of not knowing where she is, of not being able to pick up a phone and just say 'hello how are you?'

Even from a safety point of view, if no one was looking for Alicia then she would have been totally alone and if anything did happen to her it would have been months or years before her family found out.

Each night before I went to bed, I revised my map and planned my next day's tasks. What areas I was going to cover, what churches and hostels I would visit. I had ruled out sightseeing as being one of her reasons for visiting Paris and as such these areas did not consume my search.

I also phoned hostels and asked if Alicia had reserved a bed or had checked in. Some assisted me with information, others told me that they could not give out that information, those hostels I had to personally visit.

Some hostels were part of a group and they offered to email the posters to other member hostels, which saved a lot of leg work.

Each day, I walked from around 7.30 am until around 2 am. Then I would sit in the lobby of my hostel for around an hour while planning the next day's itinerary. I was barely getting three to four hours sleep per day. My dreaming would also help steer me in my chosen search locations. The vastness of the city would often distract me when hope faded. But hope itself provided the strength and resolute that I needed to continue.

Below is my map of areas covered during the search. However for your own search, and God forbid that you are ever in that position, I would recommend that you take photos of the streets that you search from day one. Even purchase an ordnance survey map of the city. And if there is more than one of you searching then this must be coordinated so that you cover more ground without any undue duplication.

Each night the map would sit on the table, I would stare at it becoming increasingly despaired. Paris was huge, why did I ever think that I could do this? I can't let everyone down. But at times I was consumed with many negative feelings? So many areas, so many streets, but which ones do I pick? Hostels and religious sights were my first choice. I would research hostels and churches from the internet on my laptop then plot them on my map for my next morning's journey.

It is estimated that there are 197 churches in Paris. The oldest church is Saint-Germain-des-Prés built in the sixth century. There were hundreds of hostels and thousands of streets. The pure size of the search area was insurmountable and that was assuming Alicia had remained in Paris and indeed still within the city.

Thomas Jefferson said that, *"A walk about Paris will provide lessons in history, beauty, and in the point of Life."* Well for sure I was getting to walk around Paris but could not indulge in its beauty, I had no time. And my point in life at this particular time was to make sure Alicia was found safe and well. The history and beauty of Paris would have to wait for another time, but I'm sure it would be a lovely place to visit under different circumstances.

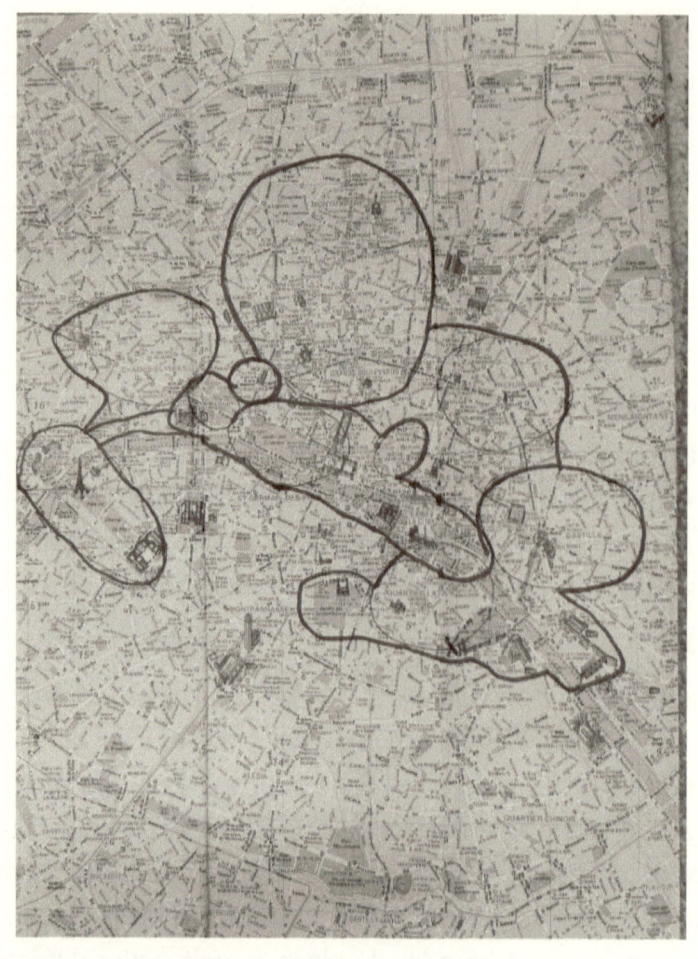

**Thousands of people go missing in Paris each year, many are found, but the police and the authorities can't find everyone, they need your eyes to.**

# Each morning began with Hope

# Each night ended with despair

# Where was Alicia?

Nights and days began to blend into each other, my strategy was not to waver from my original program of looking for Alicia. While it was not yet producing results, I needed this structure in order to maintain my faith and hope of finding Alicia. Again I was making the assumption that she was still in Paris.

The fact that I made myself believe that I would find Alicia on day one began to eat into me. This was certainly not a realistic goal for anyone to achieve. I would suggest that anyone searching for a missing person creates achievable goals. Certainly the overall goal is to find the missing person. However, smaller measurable and achievable goals such as, creating posters and distribution, searching specific areas or buildings, enlisting help from other people, visiting places that the missing might be interested about and so forth, these type of goals can help your mental health.

I had made a list of what my days would entail. And had already decided that those goals would only be changed if I had an epiphany or received any other valuable information that was worthy of exploring.

At this stage, I had no idea what Alicia was going through. But I did understand the worry, the uncertainty and the feeling of hopelessness that her family were enduring. Put yourself in their shoes, how would you feel?

The world can be a great place, but it can also be a dangerous place and when you are in a country that is not your native speaking country, it can become fraught with language and freedom barriers. People with another agenda can take advantage of the vulnerable and their current position.

A vulnerable person can be defined as a youth, teenager, homeless person (young and old), someone suffering with mental health issues, or a person in a bad place in their life's emotions. Sometimes a person can be unknowingly forced into a circle of trafficking and kidnap by choice. (Initially they were unaware of what was about to befall them and were taken in with another person's false claims of help and false goodwill, and then then become kidnapped or trafficked, with little hope of escaping)

When you are in a bad place or become vulnerable by sleeping on the streets or have limited cash or food, you are more open to accepting dysfunctional help. These offers of help are masked from the real reason, and often a person can be introduced into slave labour or sexual exploitation. And once you find yourself in that domain, it becomes very hard to escape. In most cases drugs or other threats keep a person locked into their abduction.

An extract from an article written by social worker Victoria VanTol highlights the urgent need for government assistance to halt homelessness and poverty. *"Studies suggests that 19-40% of youth and young adults who experience homelessness become victims of human trafficking. It happens in big cities and rural communities, and it happens to both boys and girls."* This percentage rises when you include people with depression or mental health issues.

As such this was another urgent reason for finding Alicia, to ensure that she did not fall prey to this degenerated part of society where human beings take advantage of people in vulnerable positions. These degenerates are a curse to society and a threat to your family and as such must be stopped in their tracks.

However, it has now become a multibillion pound industry and encompasses wealth and people in power. The news has outlined the case of Jeffrey Epstein and his trafficking and paedophile network. His wealth allowed him the freedom and security to prey on young vulnerable girls. But what is sad, despite all of his connections with the rich and famous coming to and forth from his home, and a home that was filled with young girls. No other major prosecutions have unfolded.

This begs one to wonder, how many people that are famous, wealthy or in a position of authority have had their connections with Epstein covered up? Most people have read stories, interviews and research about Prince Andrew, yet he still walks free without any formal charges despite the allegations along together with all the other rich and famous people that have been part of this triangulation of abuse.

Even despite victims providing factual testimony about certain individuals involved, prosecutions have all about dried up. If we look at the recent developments in the USA regarding the murder of George Lloyd and the policemen who did this terrible deed. We can clearly see a resemblance to the Epstein case. Racism in this day and age still exists, likewise the wealthy think that they can get away with atrocities without any recourse of justice.

As you can see if a person goes missing they can easily become integrated into this underground network of abuse. And it's led by some people in power of authority and the wealthy. Perhaps the authorities should be taking a closer look at those with an unjustifiable amount of wealth. There were many times I hoped that Alicia did not fall prey to such people, and with Alicia's lack of money she was an ideal candidate for such organisations or individuals.

# False Alarm

One of my daily rituals was making phone calls to hostels that were outside my search map. It was physically impossible for one person to visit every hostel and I certainly did not have the time to do so either. As such I would try and phone these hostels to ensure I was covering most of Paris.

On one of these phone conversations, the person hesitated after I gave him Alicia's description. He then asked me to hold while he checked with a supervisor. On his return he informed me that he could not say yes or no to my question.

At first I thought, fantastic Alicia is at this hostel. I asked the desk clerk several other questions, but our conversation began to go around in circles. This hostel was quite a distance away from the city centre and I did not want to waste time on a wild goose chase. So I thought I would give him the opportunity to answer a question without actually saying she was there. I asked him,

"Would it be beneficial if I came to the hostel?"

He replied, "It might be?"

Fantastic, I have found Alicia. I quickly mapped my route to the hostel, and began my underground and walking journey that took well over one hour to eventually get there. Plus I made several frustrating wrong turns. However, in the scheme of things these wrong turns might have been productive, but unfortunately they were not. I had configured my mind-set to look at such situations as opportunities rather than a waste of time, regardless of how they pan out. By keeping an open mind to all the failures in my search stopped negativity from taking over. Thus hope and positivity go hand in hand towards keeping you sane.

Out of breath, roasting hot and stinking of sweat I finally arrived at the correct hostel. I began to recap our previous conversation while showing him Alicia's photograph. I explained that he gave me hope that a women of that description was staying at their hostel. He replied, "Oh No, it's just that I could not give you any information out over the phone."

I thought it is absolutely pointless arguing with him, which is actually what I wanted to do over a miscommunication between us. So I remained calm and let my frustration go. I left him details and a poster of Alicia. Getting Alicia back was more important that creating a pointless argument and alienating one less person looking for her. I needed all the allies I could muster.

What you have to remember, is while a situation like this is frustrating, it may be an opportunity that you would not have normally taken. And perhaps one that could yield something positive. So my frustration did not last long, as I took the positive from that journey.

The Hostel list below was given to me by Antonio before they left Paris. They had already began to check the ones marked with an X. I subsequently added many others to this list, you don't realise how many hostels there are in Paris until you actually start to list them. So many and so little time.

| | Date | | 08H00 | 14H30 |
|---|---|---|---|---|
| X | BVJ OPERA | 01 42 36 88 18 | | |
| | MIJE | 01 42 74 23 45 | | |
| X | St CHRIS CANAL | 01 40 34 34 40 | | |
| X | St CHRIS GDN | 01 70 08 52 22 | | |
| | OT CDG 1 | 01 74 25 04 70 | | |
| | OT CDG 2 | 01 74 25 04 75 | | |
| | OT ORLY | 01 74 22 11 41 | | |
| | Espace Tourisme | 01 70 03 15 14 | | |
| X | Le Village | 01 42 64 22 02 | | |
| X | Vintage | 01 40 16 16 40 | | |
| | 3 Ducks | 01 48 42 04 05 | | |
| | Les Piaules | 01 43 55 09 97 | | |
| | Oops | 01 47 07 47 00 | | |
| | Caulaincourt | 01 46 06 46 06 | | |
| | Montclair | 01 46 06 46 07 | | |
| X | Le D'artagnan | 01 40 32 34 56 | | |
| | Jules Ferry | 01 43 57 55 60 | | |
| | Auberge Internationale | 01 47 00 62 00 | | |
| | CISP | 01 44 75 60 04 | | |
| | FIAP | 01 43 13 17 00 | | |
| | Arty Hostel | 01 40 34 40 34 | | |
| | Smart Hostel | 01 48 78 25 15 | | |
| | ENJOY HOSTEL | 01 45 40 99 48 | | |
| | Young and Happy | 01 47 07 47 07 | | |
| | Perfect Hostel | 01 42 81 18 86 | | |

# Emotional Rollercoaster

As each night came to a close, so did my hope. I struggled with my emotions and spoke with tears in my eyes to Sofia. Talking with Sofia each day, helped ease the stress I was going through. I don't think that helped her, but Sofia wanted to be strong for our children, herself and me. This was Toxic Stress for everyone and my, 'fight or flight' mode was in constant overdrive. My emotional release was with speaking with her. Sofia listened and gave me encouragement without lowering my self-esteem any further. Without this form of resilience, I would have surely floundered in my own bucket of self-depression.

Moreover, I was also aware of what Sofia would have being going through, with her niece missing and me going through hell trying to find her. As a result I was excessively reluctant to tell her everything that was going through my mind. I could not do that to her. So our discussions would be on topics like where I was searching, to the fun stuff like the number of chapels I had been inside (more in the last week than the last forty years,☺) to how our kids were getting on at school and to how Sofia was doing. It's important to discuss normal day to day things and events… that helped elevate a lot of my stress.

Little did I know that Sofia was also going through her own problems with unnecessary and stressful discussions with her family?

Each night before I went to sleep, it was important for me that I planned my next day's tasks. By doing so it gave me resilience for having hope and a plan of action for the next day ahead. It meant I could get out of bed with hope and follow my plan of action for that day. Of course there were always alterations to the daily plan as the day proceeded.

Scan the QR code below to go to the goodtherapy.org website that provides 9 pointers towards helping you when you feel as if you are on a roller coaster of emotions.

I like the song by Vivian Green, Emotional Rollercoaster

# Notre Dame

Image by Ian Kelsall at Pixabay

This was one of the many religious site that I visited looking for Alicia

Notre Dame, famous for being a religious and tourist attraction. How sad when it burnt down. However, what is even sadder was the many people announcing how they were donating millions to get it built to its former glory within five years.

**No money for the ordinary person, how sick is that?**

Extract from Catholic News Agency *"Some of the major donors who have pledged the most money include French billionaire Francois-Henri Pinault, who pledged 100 million euros, and Bernard Arnault, who pledged 200 million euros, according to an NPR report. The owners of L'Oréal cosmetic company along with the Bettencourt Schueller Foundation pledged 200 million euros."*

What about the missing?

What about opening religious buildings to help put a roof over the heads of the homeless at night?

What about religion actually doing something constructive with their assets of billions, people in poverty need that money and help?

Why are they not rebuilding humanity? Humanity for people in need, people sick, people missing, people living on the streets, people in poverty and so forth?

The sheer vastness of the money these businesses and millionaires are donating could help end homelessness in Paris and many other major cities overnight.

I suggest that the money they are donating should be used to build a homeless shelter bang right in the middle of the ashes of Notre Dame. Then, and only then will religion gain one ounce of respect from me.

The time for change is now, the time for telling religion to actually put people first, to ensure pure equality in every fabric of life, is now!

The only true faith/religion, is that of humanity, dignity, freedom and pure equality. Now that is a religion worthy of worshipping.

# Hope

**H**ope is what I awoke with every morning, this provided me with the strength to continue searching for Alicia.

*Hope is the thing with feathers that perches in the soul and sings the tune without the words and never stops at all.*

*(Emily Dickinson an American Poet)*

HOPE is one of the three theological virtues of the Christian religion, alongside faith and love.

HOPE is mentioned in the Holy Bible. But HOPE is also a part of every person on earth, regardless if they believe in religion or not. HOPE is what gives us faith from adversity towards that of dignity and freedom from exploitation, harm or abuse.

My own personal hope saying and indeed one that has given me faith throughout the years, it is a sign that I received when I had adversity in my life. This sign of hope came from a neon sign in an underground station. When I was going through adversity in my life something inside my head told me to stop walking and to look up, and this is what I saw when I did.

### "There is Light at the End of the Tunnel"

Positive voices in my head helped me heal. But, I cannot overemphasize the need for HOPE. Without hope you are destined for failure and a spiral downwards until you reach the pit of depression. This sign helped me immensely when I was going through a period of adversity, even today when things go bad, I recall that sign and it helps ease my pain and gives me the strength to keep going, it became my rainbow. Even in times of despair, my rainbow is the sign below.

# There is Light at the End of the Tunnel.

# Finding Hope through Song:

## With the Missing People Choir

## I Hope - Missing People Choir and Friends

Each morning I awoke with a sense of HOPE, and during the day when my hope was faltering I phoned Sofia for an update of what was going on back in normality. I also stuck to my plan of action, and that bolstered me up for searching for that needle in a haystack within the vastness of Paris.

I reminded myself throughout this search that my biggest asset and my worst asset are one of the same…and that is "**I never give up**".

Each night I stayed in a different hostel, just in the hope that I saw Alicia or someone who had seen her in their travels. I wanted to sleep in places that Alicia could possibly still afford to stay in. Every day I returned to the hostel she had met her mum, Antonio and the police in the hope she returned. Something inside me, a feeling made me believe that she liked it here.

I was also making one huge assumption and that was Alicia had remained in Paris, effectively putting all my eggs into one basket. After meeting her mum Alicia could possibly have left Paris or moved to the outskirts of the city just to ensure that she wasn't found again.

Wednesday evening the 26th September: Alma (Alicia's sister) and her dad Luis had arrived in Paris and began to search for her. I got Luis's phone number and texted him about meeting up to discuss where I have covered and what we could do next etc. However, we never did meet up as they were heading to the outskirts of Paris to speak with Father Andre that next morning.

## Our text messages

Thursday 27th September, Alma (txt): we're still waiting on word, I'm now staying till Sunday, so I will more than likely meet up on Saturday or Sunday cover more ground for now, I might be staying with Father Andre from tomorrow onwards so if Alicia contacts him we will be there, thanks again for all your help.

Mario (txt) that sounds like a good plan hopefully Alicia will make contact with Father Andre and you will be there. I wish I could do more.

Friday 28th September at 10.45am Alma (txt): sorry I'm only getting back to you now, my mum wants me to come home today she doesn't want me and dad wandering around here, you've done so much and at least we know that she is safe, she's not in any hospitals and the police are sure to come across something sometime, thank you for trying your best x

Mario (txt): hi Alma, have a safe flight. Your mum is just worried about you, which is what mums do. It's a stressful time for you all. I'm flying back on Sunday, so if you have any ideas of where to look let me know. I'm at staying at same place Alicia stayed previously for tonight and tomorrow, and will look at hostels, chapels and parks, take care.

Alma (txt): that's great, I think she might be at Sunday mass at Saint Nicholas church on le Bourget, she asked Father Andre about mass times and she hasn't been there since she arrived so I think that could be worth a try, I'm meeting with Father Andre soon so I will let you know what time masses are, I know and I'm going to do what I'm told for now don't need my mum stressing out more than she is, thanks again Mario, we appreciate your help.

Mario (txt): it's no problem at all, over last few days I've been checking out mass in some of the local chapels, but there are so many, many chapels.

Alma (txt): aye I was trying to check them out myself to be at the right one at the right time seems nearly impossible but I think Saint Nicolas on Sunday is a good a guess as any

Mario (txt): Yeh I think so as well, hopefully she will go back there.

Thursday morning arrived and they went to be with Father Andre in the hope that Alicia would turn up there. I began my journey to go meet them. I had just arrived at the train station when I received a phone call from Laura asking me not to go up to Fathers David's, she said it would be a waste of time us all being up there. I agreed.

After that phone call, I sat on a stone seat and for some reason began to doubt myself. However, I needed the rest so I sat there for an hour watching the thousands of people pass by. I sat there hoping to catch a glimpse of Alicia making her way from the subway to the train on her route to see Father Andre. I began to put the doubting feeling behind me and hope returned. Perhaps this was a necessary sign and process for me to go through in my journey to find Alicia?

I had a few false alarms with girls that looked similar to Alicia, but unfortunately none were her. I had sat for long enough, it was time to make a move, so I got up and began my journey of searching for Alicia with a renewed enthusiasm and determination. It was if I had sensed that Alicia was not going to turn up at Fathers Andres church.

I never did get up to meet with Father Andre's, but I also believed for some reason that she would not go back there. But it was good that Alma and her Dad where there just in case.

# Come Back to Spain

Antonio and Laura phoned me around 10pm on Thursday night (27th September 2019) and insisted that I come home. They said that they would book me a Friday morning flight, [I think that was to ensure that I did come home.] I told them *"No, it was ok, I am on my way back to my hostel and I'll book the flight myself when I get back"*. Sofia then phoned and said that she was speaking with Laura and that I should come back home. Likewise, I also told Sofia that I would book a flight when I got back to my hostel.

I took the phone calls quite bad, I felt that everyone had no faith in me or that I was hopeless and had no chance of finding Alicia. So for a short period of time, I was confused, bewildered and upset, the stress of searching for Alicia was uncontrollably taking its toll on me and perhaps distorting my reasoning abilities.

Why the phone calls now? Did they think that Alicia was Ok, and it was pointless looking for her? I don't know? Or could they sense that I was on a pathway to hell, I have no idea? As I said before, one of my strengths is also my weakness, **"I never give up"**.

However, as I walked back towards my hostel, I remembered some other places that I had missed on my daily plan. So I walked to those places and fulfilled my daily plan, by the time I got back to the hostel it was after 1am. I sat in the lobby and connected to their Wi-Fi and browsed the flights home, but I couldn't face to book any. I was definitely not ready to leave Paris. I knew in my heart that Alicia needed help, and I could not have looked myself in the mirror if I was to leave Paris without finding her. After all that was what I came to Paris to do.

Day 8, Friday morning at 7am and for the first time I got up without a plan, turned on my computer to book my flight...But I still couldn't do it.

Sitting there with another coffee in hand, [And I had given up drinking coffee around six months prior...but since I met Laura and Antonio on my first morning in Paris coffee had become my comfort drink]

I made my decision which was, "I'm not ready to leave Paris." I phoned Sofia and told her that I was not coming back as I could not get on any flights until Sunday (Yes, I lied). I called Alicia's mum and told her that I was going to stay a bit longer in Paris.

Later that afternoon I thought I better phone Sofia and tell her the truth and that I had lied to her, just in case Laura phoned her first. I wasn't ready to leave, I was not ready to go back home without finding Alicia. Sofia agreed that I should stay, though she was worried about me and how I was coping. And to be honest, I wasn't coping well. I now felt that I was failing everyone and my mental health began to falter. But Alicia deserved to be found, and I was damn well going to find her.

Deep inside I knew things were not ok with Alicia. You don't agree to meet your mother, then disappear without any discussion. Do you? That did not add up, something must be wrong, why would Alicia just not turn up and disappear yet again? I could not release that idea from my mind.

Despite my frustration, I still felt that I was here for a reason and regardless of how I felt mentally, I was not ready to give up. I also knew that by staying I was setting myself up for a possible larger and more consequential failure, and God knows what that would have done to me and my family. But really you can't give up on hope. Every minute I remained in Paris was a step closer in fulfilling the goal of finding Alicia or so I had convinced myself.

That feeling was also another part of my resilience programme against any possible mental health issues that could arise from the search. I held tight to HOPE, so I couldn't give up on my search, I still felt I could make a difference being here in Paris. To me going home now would have taken me down a darker pathway, I therefore decided to stay until I was ready to leave Paris or financially broke, whichever came first. By giving myself that objective I was protecting myself from my own mental health failure.

By Friday morning, my feet and legs were in sheer agony, I could hardly walk for the pain and for the first time in my life I actually felt my age, it was the first time I had 'hobbled along' in my lifetime.

By Friday the 26th of September, late afternoon, I had put in place an infrastructure for Alicia. I had a choice of short term studio apartments for Alicia, a female contact that she could speak to whenever Alicia would need her assistance. All I had to do now was find Alicia. However, I'm sure that her family would have preferred her to come back home rather than stay in Paris, but that would have been Alicia's choice.

I met Aurnia on my search journey a day after I had arrived in Paris, she was working in an Irish pub. When I showed her the missing poster, Aurnia said that she knew of Alicia and that she got information from her friends about Alicia via her Facebook page. Aurnia's friends back in Spain knew Alicia, they all went to the same University. It sure was a small world after all. Aurnia was extremely helpful, and gave me advice on areas where teenagers would hang out in Paris. So I had added those places to my search map.

I was also looking for short to long term accommodation in Paris and Aurnia provided me with the details of a website that many use in Paris, see below: And I managed to get a studio apartment on hold.

https://www.pap.fr Rent (English) = Location (in French)

Paris 6e

Appartement 1 pièce 9 m²
520 €

Paris 15e

Appartement 1 pièce 19 m²
720 €

# Sacré-Cœur

On Friday night I went to Sacré-Cœur, the church on the hill, mass was at 10 pm. I had been there before, but for some reason I was drawn back there tonight. I walked around all the hundreds of young people sitting on the slope towards the church looking for Alicia in the dim light. This was a hangout for the local youths, they were sitting drinking, smoking and having a laugh. I had hoped to find Alicia on the slopes or at the mass later. The Basilica of the Sacred Heart of Paris, was commonly known as Sacré-Cœur Basilica, it is a Roman Catholic Church and minor basilica. It is dedicated to the Sacred Heart of Jesus in Paris. Locals, tourists and religious pilgrims visited this church in their masses.

I took these photographs on my first visit to the church. I searched around the area several times. Laura had suggested that Alicia might speak to the nuns here with the view of getting work and accommodation.

On Friday night I walked around the nearby area and found some interesting restaurants, bars and artists.

I sat outside one of the many bar/restaurants while waiting for mass to begin in an hour's time. And for the first time since being in Paris I actually sat down and came to a point of peace within myself. For the first time since being in Paris I had a feeling of tranquillity and true hope. I relaxed and sat on a seat outside a bar with a glass of beer and some peanuts. I sat there observing all the people walking past. Singers and artists all doing their bit of making a living while entertaining the tourists and locals.

Mass was about to start and at one with myself I left the bar and headed towards the gates of the church. Security checked everyone's bags as they entered the area surrounding the church. I walked around the packed pews diligently looking at everyone, but Alicia was not to be found.

After mass I spoke with a priest but he did not recognise the girl in the photograph. Then he introduced me to a nun that was responsible for getting work for young girls. I showed the nun the photograph of Alicia, but unfortunately she said she had never come across her either. However, I was a bit sceptical, for some reason I don't believe the nun would have told me otherwise. After all in most countries and in particularly France, an adult can choose to disappear and at nineteen years of age Alicia was an adult in their minds.

After our talk I returned inside and lit a candle, I also looked through their visitor's book of messages. I wrote a message, and I was a bit fluxed as I thought that I would have found her there tonight. *"Alicia if you see this, please contact your family we all love and miss you"* ☺

While I was sitting at the bar, I contemplated getting one of the caricature artists to do a drawing of Alicia and to leave it there, asking if anyone had seen this person. But I did not. As you can see my mind was wrestling with any idea to help find her.

I left the church and walked back to my new hostel for a change of clothes before I began my search. Earlier that afternoon when checking in, I met a really nice and thoughtful teenager, same age as Alicia. Ethan had cycled all the way from Norway. He was one of my three other roommates in my hostel dorm. That night I arrived back earlier than normal, and we all chatted away for a good while. This was great as it grounded me and lowered my stress, we talked about anything and everything. I even had a laugh or two, I needed this time-out to refocus, and it gave me the strength to continue my search.

69 | Missing in Paris - Hope and Resilience

# Day 8 Saturday's Breakfast
## 29th September 2018

In the morning, I got up early as usual, most people were still asleep. I had breakfast and researched some ideas on my laptop for over an hour. I took longer than normal, I was beginning to relax, and I needed this time for myself. I began to see a light at the end of the tunnel, I became relaxed and hopeful. I was about to leave, when I spotted Ethan having his breakfast in another part of the many different areas of the breakfast room, it was near the coffee bar.

While I was eager to get out and begin my search for Alicia, a sign encouraged me not to leave just yet but rather to go join Ethan for a chat. He was a nice lad full of enthusiasm, and boy did I need some enthusiasm in my life right now.

I grabbed another coffee and we sat and chatted for a while. It was great having that normal day to day conversation, this interaction helped to ease my stress and reduced the anxiety that my body had built during my five days of being in Paris.

Ethan offered to give me his bicycle for my search. However, the backs of my feet were too sore to pedal so I declined his offer. Ethan couldn't take his bike with him on his return journey to Norway as it would cost him too much money in air fares. I told him to sell his bike and get some extra cash for his trip back home and that I would keep my eye out for shops looking to buy bikes.

Unfortunately, I never did get to tell him of a place I had found. Neither did I get the chance to thank him or to wish him bon voyage. The short time that I met and spoke with Ethan provided me with a boost of compassion and hope that lit up my life.

Moments like this give you hope that the human race are human after all. And when a teenager offers you his own assets to help find a lost one, well that in itself is better than any prayer.

# The cross to bear
## Saturday 29th of September 2018

That time I spent having breakfast with Ethan was the deciding factor of finding Alicia. Finding that needle in a haystack, had come true.

In fact I offer my sincere gratitude to Ethan, for he managed to restore faith in me when I needed it the most. Not only that, if I had not changed my plan and talked with him, I would not have found Alicia. So thanks', very…very much Ethan. You are a true young gentleman.

As I went to leave the breakfast room, I saw a girl sitting on a chair in a corner with her head held downwards. I went over to see if she was ok. As I approached her I could not believe my eyes. I was overjoyed, ecstatic, it was Alicia I had found her safe and well. Alicia looked up, I had a grin on my face about a mile long. She stood up hurriedly, we hugged briefly and I said that I was so glad to see her. She instantly responded "my mum knows I am here, so it's ok"

Half expecting the same enthusiasm back, I was stunned when I was then met with a forced-smile and the words "I have to go now, I have lots to do" She walked past me, I asked her to speak with me just for a few minutes, but she turned and kept walking while saying "I have to go," I pleaded several times to keep her near me, using every excuse I could muster, but she was having none of it, Alicia clearly wanted to leave and get on with whatever she had to do.

She initially appeared ok, but I could sense from her actions that all was far from right.

Alicia left, and I quickly hobbled to get my laptop, phone and bag. But by the time I got outside of the hostel I couldn't see Alicia anywhere, I looked up and down several streets and now I began to panic. How I could I find her and lose her so quickly?

I hobbled along Rue de la Tour des Dames, my eyes frantically scurrying in every direction, finally I spotted Alicia in the distance crossing in-between parked cars. I limped as I ran, as fast as I could, up a small hill and frantically trying to catch up with her.

When I finally caught up, I remained a good distance away, not to far but far enough not to be noticed. After the panic was over I phoned Alicia's mum and Antonio to let them know I've found her and to get over to Paris as soon as they could. I phoned Sofia and briefly brought her up to date with the news. She too was over the moon.

With each minute that I followed Alicia my heart sank deeper and deeper into despair. I could feel the pain that she was feeling. I wanted to go to her and help her, but I could not risk losing Alicia before her family arrived. I contended myself in following her and making sure she was safe until her family arrived.

As time passed painfully slow, it became obvious that Alicia had a mental health issue. I was devastated, I came to Paris believing that when Alicia was found I could help her to come home or to ensure she was safe remaining in Paris. Now I was faced with the task of following a teenager who was in severe pain internally and externally.

When I was looking for Alicia I was drawn to certain areas that I would pass every day. I was drawn to a district of Paris, but I didn't know why? However, now that I was following Alicia I discovered she walked past some of the same streets that I had searched on. It was uncanny how out of the thousands of streets in Paris, I kept being drawn to streets that Alicia was walking past today. We might even have passed each other without noticing in those four days of searching. There were so many people walking on both sides of the streets, it was impossible to look at every person.

So I had to be specific to what I was looking for. I was looking for Alicia as per the description I had received of what she was wearing at the time of her disappearance. That allowed me to whittle the search down. I was looking for a blonde hair girl, with black jeans and black converse boots. So I scanned the crowds for that description, which allowed me to focus on a smaller amount of people out of the crowds of thousands. If she had dyed her hair then I guess my search would have been flawed.

Alicia was walking slowly with her head bent downwards towards the ground. When she came to an obstacle such as a tree with a perimeter of stones around it. Alicia would walk directly up to the first part of the obstacle, stop or slow down, turn and walk along the edge and would continue to adjust her turns until she was back on course again. And always with her head bend downwards and never looking up.

Every now and again she would stop and begin bowing and blessing objects, to me it appeared to be random blessings as not all objects were the same. However, I'm sure that Alicia had her reasons for picking such places for her blessings. Alicia walked continuously, stopping for a minute or two only to write in a diary that she kept in her pocket.

Alicia was now hobbling along, her feet obviously sore from all the walking she had undoubtedly done since arriving in Paris. Some people would turn and stare at her, only a handful of people actual asked if she was ok. If you were a person walking past her, you would definitely know that she was not ok.

I kept everyone informed back home, but I mostly only cried when I spoke to Sofia, I had to be strong when speaking with Alicia's Mum and Antonio. To watch Alicia go through this torture was soul destroying. To stand back and not be able to help was sending me to the pits of hell. I was walking behind her with tears streaming from my eyes. All I wanted to do was to give Alicia a hug and reassure her that I was here for her and that her family missed and loved her. But that was not an option for consideration. If I did go to her then she could easily have fled, and in her state of mind god forbid what could have happened next.

Alicia was not concerned about traffic lights and would get impatient waiting to cross, she never looked up to see what colour the traffic light was. She appeared to either gauge her time for crossing as when others crossed or by randomly crossing regardless of the lights showing STOP.

To keep Alicia safe when we approached traffic lights I moved up to her left and literally jumped out when she went to cross the road, while raising and waving my hands in the air trying to stop the cars from hitting her. I was met with tooting of horns and drivers waving their fists at me, but hey that was a small price to pay for her safety.

# Man dressed in Black Jeans

As I continued to follow Alicia, several men approached her, thankfully most moved on when she waved them away which she did so without lifting her head to look at them.

But, there was one man who wasn't going to give up that easy, he was skinny and slightly taller in height to Alicia, he wore black jeans, white trainers and a black bomber jacket. He persistently spoke to Alicia who was walking in a hobbling and crippling manner, her head now held even lower towards the ground than before.

He spoke in French until he realised that she spoke English. Then the words of 'come with me, I will help you' became a ritual of deception towards someone interested in achieving their own means.

Alicia waved her hands many times to dismiss this man from pestering her. But he remained tight by her side as they walked. He followed her wherever she went. Passers-by looked on at a young girl who obviously needed assistance, but instead went on their own business without intervening. Indeed this man was so vigorous in his tactics to persuade Alicia to come with him that he did not even notice me following behind.

This is typical of people who assume that the person with her is a boyfriend or…? People are afraid to ask *'are you OK? Is that person with you, are they bothering you, do you need any help?'* [Scan the QR Code to hear an uplifting story, of Intervention]

However in this instance it would have made no difference. If you had asked Alicia, her reply would have been "I am ok, now leave me alone please." Now what can you say to that? Especially when it is a stranger asking the questions and you really do not know that person. You have to therefore assume that she is ok and perhaps she is going through a bad phase. Or do you?

Again the frustration, as a stranger what would you do if you came across a girl similar to Alicia walking with a man constantly in her face?

Would you take the time to observe and see if she was in danger?

Would you just glance and then walk on?

Would you phone the police and ask for their assistance?

**What would you do?**

Alicia walked all day without anyone contacting the police or authorities, yet she was displaying all the signs of something being wrong. Phoning the police was not an option for me, she had already fooled them once before.

Shadowing Alicia with this man following her was taking its toll on Alicia and me, I couldn't approach her otherwise she would have known that I was following her, and she could have done a runner. At the same time how could I let this man pester her? Catch 22 situation. However, my mind was already decided, first and foremost I needed to make sure I kept Alicia in my sights. Secondly, If Alicia was in harm's way, then I would intervene. Thirdly, I would choose my time and place to stop him if it continued much longer.

I was resolute in my decision only to intervene if absolutely necessary, or if she was in immediate danger.

What I was concerned with: In Alicia's state of mind it would have taken only a split second for any accomplice to pull up in a car or van, there would have been no struggle, Alicia was weak with walking constantly and had a definite lack of nourishment. With these thoughts my distance between Alicia and this man became less, just in case I had to act quickly.

Alicia and her stalker were approaching a metro entrance, he was on her left hand side and Alicia was nearest to the roadside. As they arrived at the entrance, she stepped down the stairs while he kept on walking to the left without going down into the subway. At first I thought shit! I can't lose her in the underground, I ran to make sure I was next to her. Alicia put her hand in her pocket, probably looking for a ticket, and I was preparing to jump over the barrier, but luckily she had no ticket. Alicia turned around and nearly banged into me, I turned and twisted to the side and faced the wall so she would not recognise me.

As she was walking up the stairs Alicia's stalker was coming down towards her. She walked straight past him and he turned with his arms stretched out to grasp her. I ran up the stairs and pushed him up against the wall and whispered, 'leave her alone, and stay away'. I let him go and moved to his right past him only to be pulled by the side of my hoodie, which send me spinning around. As I spun around his other fist came towards me, luckily as I spun around my arm blocked his punch to my stomach. I kicked out to loosen his grip on my hoodie. He fell and rolled down the stairs, he instantly got up, ran and jumped the barrier to the subway. Thankfully, that was the last we saw of him.

I ran up the stairs to the outside of the metro entrance and couldn't see Alicia anywhere, there were several roads to choose from. Luckily a few seconds later I spotted her walking towards a bench on the pavement. She was about one hundred feet away and by this stage it was obvious that she had no intention of looking behind her to see if anyone was following, so I decided to stay closer to her from now on.

# Crying Shame

Alicia sat on the bench and put her head on her knees while her hands covered the side of her head. The position that everyone's puts themselves in when overly stressed. The tears were flowing from her eyes so much so that I could clearly see her tears hit the dry hot ground.

She was in pain both internally and externally. I joined her in crying from a short distance, such a caring, nice and beautiful young girl, how can she be allowed to suffer so much and why?

Alicia had been enrolled in university, but drink, drugs and partying took their toll on her and led her brain on a journey that no person should have to endure. She had just dropped out of her university course a couple of months prior to disappearing to Paris.

All these factors of stress can become a lethal cocktail that can fuck with your brain. Suddenly all your despairs and adversities are soon uncovered from the past and merge with your present and future expectations and this begins their journey to destroy you.

Teenage years can be hard and they do suffer just like adults do. Take a moment to try and recall your teenage years, how did you feel, how did others make you feel. Did you struggle too much with exams or what you wanted to do in life?

I stood helplessly and watched Alicia suffer, all on her own. That memory and that pain will always be a reminder and a thought that perhaps I could have done better for Alicia. Sofia and my family were my shoulder to cry on. Sometimes I just phoned home to hear their voices, other times to update them. But Alicia had no one when she cried, her only friend was her diary that she wrote in. She was suffering alone believing that her God was directing her. Watching Alicia's despair was insurmountable on my wellbeing, but I did not care about myself, I just wanted Alicia to be safe and well again.

I began to feel her pain myself and all I wanted to do was stop the pain that she was enduring. But I was helpless to do that for her.

# Café's

After, a few minutes Alicia got up and continued to walk. Several times over the next two hours she would sit down, on street benches, or on the ground or seats outside café's (not drinking or eating anything), she would take out her diary and add some more writings. Every time she did this there were always tears flowing from her eyes. Sometimes she would read a book that she carried in her pocket, later I found out that it was a religious book.

Alicia stopped and looked inside a bar/cafe, presumably deciding if she should go in. She went inside and I stood outside and I walked past the doors every now and again just to make sure she was still in there and all was ok. She had a coffee and another drink from the bar. Not sure what it was? Perhaps a liquor of some sort. She left her table to go to the bathroom, afterwards she walked straight out the door without paying. The bar tender ran outside after her, but I managed to stop him as he went to pass me. I paid him and apologised, he was quite happy that he got paid and went back inside without any fuss.

I continued to follow Alicia. I had already made my mind up that I wasn't going to eat or drink, as how could I stop and use a bathroom without losing sight of Alicia? Plus my daughter is always screaming at me "Dad how long are you going to be in the toilet?" When that thought popped into my head it brought a smile to my dreary face and a momentous break from the reality that I now found myself in.

How naive I was before I left Barcelona. I persuaded myself that I could make sure Alicia was Ok and that I would put in place an infrastructure for her in Paris. Well even the thoughts of that infrastructure was now crumbling into the abyss of a false reality. Alicia needed help.

The Café/Bar that Alicia had her short stop at.

# The Bus Stop

Alicia carried on her ritual of walking in a set pattern while stopping to bless objects, and to read from her book or to write in her diary. It was a hot day, I was beginning to become dehydrated and I'm sure Alicia would be to. Without any food or drink apart from the coffee and liquor from the bar earlier Alicia would becoming tired and weary.

Now nature began to make its call on me, I needed the toilet, my morning's breakfast needed an exit. I had already thought about this situation, and if need be I would just have to soil myself. Not an easy thing to have to do, but rather I would have had no choice, it would have been a necessity. I was holding on hoping that Alicia would also have to make a toilet stop.

A few minutes later Alicia sat on a seat at a bus stop, I was now desperate to go to the toilet. Alicia put her bag on the seat and began to lay down, placing her head on her bag. This was my opportunity. I looked all around and there was a little takeaway on the opposite side of the road. I quickly ran over and asked if I could use their bathroom. The man said, "Only if I purchase something." So I bought a bottle of water. I thought I could get someone to pass it onto Alicia. But would you take a bottle of water from a stranger and give it to another stranger?

I had to wait my turn as someone else was in the toilet, luckily the plain glass windows of the shop allowed to me to keep an eye on Alicia and she was still laying down. I quickly went into the toilet, my daughter would have been proud of me I was in and out of the toilet in the quickest time ever in my life. Just as I left the takeaway, Alicia sat up for a minute, then stood upright putting her rucksack on her back and began her journey again.

It had been an extremely hot day, Alicia surely must be hungry and thirsty. She stopped walking and sat down on the ground about fifteen feet away from a supermarket on a corner. She pulled out her book and began to write with the same ritual of crying and tears streaming down her face. I stood at the door to the supermarket and asked a staff member near me if they could get some fruit and water and give it to the girl outside. The language barrier made it increasingly difficult for them to understand me and I wished I had paid more attention to my French lessons at school.

In the meantime a man approached Alicia and began to hassle her. I let out one almighty whistle, he looked up, and thankfully Alicia didn't. I began waving my arms and pushing my hands to the side, clearly displaying that I wanted him to leave her alone and move away. But he tried to pester her again, so I whistled again and did the same gesture with my hands.

The tall, lanky, and scruffy dressed man walked over towards me he stood directly in front twisting his face from side to side while raising his lips to display his teeth. Done as a form of intimidation and his attempt to mark his territory. He began to wave his hands in the air while screaming in French at me. Everyone in the shop stopped to take notice. I understood a couple of his words. His face came closer and I told him to back off. I remained motionless and we had a stare-off. Then he shouted a few more swear words, then turned away and walked further into the shop still shouting and throwing his long hands around in the air. As he finished his rant, Alicia stood up and began her journey. I had to leave the shop immediately without any drink or food for Alicia.

I don't believe that this man was a threat, but rather he was probably trying to get some money for food from Alicia. He looked as if he was one of the homeless that slept on a mattress or cardboard box in the doorways of Paris in the evening.

While my main concern was keeping Alicia safe, I did feel sad for this man. Society in general had let him and many others down. It would have been nice if I could have helped him.

# Help from Home

Alicia's mum and stepdad were busy trying to get a flight to Paris. However, there were no direct flights that day, so they booked a direct flight for Sunday.

In the meantime I had been keeping them informed of the mental health of Alicia. Sofia from our discussions also contacted her sister (Laura) to make sure that she understood that Alicia was not in a good mental place and indeed she needed urgent help.

Laura and Antonio were in contact with their local Politian asking for assistance and for them to speak with the foreign office in Paris again.

I had sent some photographs and a video that I had taken of Alicia to ensure that the family fully understood the reality of her mental health state and the need for urgent attention.

The wheels back home went into motion, their local Politian spoke with the foreign office in Paris and negotiations began. However, there was no assistance coming from the police. In the meantime Sofia had spoken with a friend (she works in the mental health facility at the local hospital). Sofia's friend told her to let Laura know that if she gets a letter from her doctor to show that Alicia's has mental health issues that will speed everything along. However being a weekend it was difficult to get hold of her doctor and others were reluctant to sign anything, despite the evidence being available to demonstrate that indeed Alicia needed urgent medical assistance.

In the meantime both Alicia and I were in pain from all the walking. To make things worse, I had left Spain in a hurry so only had my hard fitting office shoes with me, not too great for all the walking that was done that week. Not sure why I did not buy a pair of walking shoes when I was searching for Alicia, I had passed many shops? I think it's because I believed I did not deserve to allocate any time for myself because I hadn't found Alicia yet. Plus my days were full of searching and there was no time for anything else. [This was the wrong attitude, you really do need to take care of yourself, and I know that now.]

Their fights were booked and Laura, Antonio and Alma were due to land around 5pm on Sunday the 30th of September 2018

Their local Politian was still communicating with the foreign office officials in Spain and Paris while relaying that information back to the family.

One of the officials at the Spanish foreign office in Paris began to speak with Antonio and Laura directly. Which helped speed up the talks.

# Father Andre

Laura phoned and said that they were speaking with Father Andre, who was the priest in a parish just outside of Paris. He met with Alicia when she first arrived and according to him and the note left in her hostel room they were due to meet again, but they never did.

Alicia's parents thought that perhaps he could help, they assumed that Alicia and Father Andre had built up a relationship in the short space of time they had met.

Father Andre and my texts: (Previously in the week, 26$^{th}$ September, the morning after I had arrived in Paris.)

Mario (txt): Hi Father Andre, I'm helping Laura find Alicia and to assist in putting into place assistance for her in case she needs it. I'm not here to convince her to come home but rather put in place measures to keep her safe in the event she decides to remain here. You can get a hold of me at this number if you have any news, God bless,

Father Andre (txt): Hello Mario, thanks for your message, it's my prayer to find Alicia and try to help her. I called some Catholic Churches around yesterday to find out if they have received a young lady but no positive answer, I will also continue the search and if I meet her again I will let you know. All the best, and God bless you to. Rev, Fr Andre

Laura and Antonio suggested over several phone calls that I should approach Alicia and tell her that Father Andre has a job and a place for her to stay and that I would take her to him. However I explained that it was a bad idea. I based my decision on: a) I was physically in pain and would not have been able to make chase if she had said no and ran off. b) I was not entirely sure about Alicia and Father Andre. Since Alicia did not turn up for their pre-arranged meeting. I therefore made the decision it was not a good idea, especially being here on my own.

What I did suggest was to get Father Andre to come to us, that way I could carry on following Alicia if she decided not to go with Father Andre. They spoke to Father Andre, and I believe that he said ok. From our conversation I now believed that help from Father Andre was on its way, so I began to text Father Andre the street locations we were passing:

Saturday 29th September, (by texts from 11.23am): Mario and Father Andre

Mario: Alicia is walking along avenue de la republique

Mario: towards pere Lachaise

Mario: now walking along rue saint maur

Mario: Alicia is wearing, white shoes, dark blue jeans, grey sweatshirt and light brown bag on her back

Mario: still on rue stain maur

Mario: saint maur

Mario: still walking on rue saint maur

Father Andre: ok

Mario: passing rue de la roquette but still on saint maur

Mario: no sorry its rue leon frot

Father Andre: Am far from this route

Looking at street names in a language that I'm not used to then typing them into my phone began to be a real pain. Plus every time my eyes were away from Alicia the distance gap between us started to get longer and it was impossible to keep Father Andre and Laura updated at the same time.

So, I began to use 'WhatsApp' to take photographs of the streets that we passed and send them to Laura and Antonio. They in turn could let Father Andre know our location in Paris. This made the situation more efficient and provided accurate pronunciation of the French street names. Moreover, it allowed me to keep my eyes on Alicia at all times, it would have been too easy to lose her into streets now becoming increasingly overcrowded.

This gave me a sense of hope, at last I was going to get some assistance.

Time passed and still no sign of Father Andre, I continued to send photos of the street names. Father Andre phoned me to ask in broken English where I was now. I explained where I was and said Alicia's parents can give him full street names. He asked if I could take Alicia to him. This idea was a nonstarter. I couldn't even get Alicia to sit and talk with me for one minute never mind get her to go on a subway ride to the outskirts of Paris.

I explained to Father Andre Alicia current mental health and that she was busy doing what she needed to do, and Alicia would probably not let anything interfere with that. I asked him to phone Laura and Antonio and that they would let him know my exact location as he gets into Paris city.

A few hours passed and I was becoming frustrated at the length of time it was taking Father Andre to get to us. By this stage I really did need help, I was struggling from the pain in my feet and legs, exhaustion was beginning to take its toll, I was becoming dehydrated and the extremely hot day wasn't helping either.

However, it transpired that Father Andre was unable to travel into Paris due to other pastoral duties and a mass that he was taking would be starting soon. God forbid that the people at his mass could not understand the urgency and life threating need of a young teenager. Not only was I frustrated but I was angry at the lack of empath towards the needs of a teenager in crisis by a person of religion.

I was alone following Alicia, but the thought of someone soon being with me, gave the reassurance that I was not going to be unaided for much longer. My biggest fear was not being able to keep Alicia in my sights and losing her before her family arrived.

I hoped that I would be able to keep attentive while following her. I was knackered, the lack of sleep deprivation was beginning to make its presence well known. My food intake during that week consisted of breakfast (bread, cheese, croissants, fruit and coffee.) During the remainder of the day I would miss eating or had a quick snack or kebab and some water. This is yet another mistake, looking after yourself is vitally important, if you don't look after your own health and welfare then you could end up being useless in a continued search.

Please spare a thought and help when you can for children in poverty in other countries, if this is how I was feeling after a few days, think what these children and adults are feeling after suffering malnutrition for months or years?

The world can be a sick place. I recently read that there are 4,000 billionaires in the world. Wealth of this magnitude is sickening to the core of humanity and I do not believe for one second that such people who amass this type of wealth will be welcome into any heavenly existence.

Some of these rich throw scraps of money towards helping. But in reality no one needs so much money.

How can these people look into the mirror when there is poverty, homelessness and inequality all around us?

We need a drastic change to wealth creation and the world's current economic model, for the one we have is not working. Its model allows others to perish while the rich get richer.

# Shopping Time

The time was now around 5.30 pm, Alicia and I had walked literally nonstop around Paris for around nine hours. Alicia had nothing to eat or drink apart from the coffee and liquor. I could see that the lack of rest and nourishment was taking its toll on her to.

I forgot about the grapes that I had in my bag, I purchased earlier from a stall that we had passed. But yet again the dilemma on how to get them to Alicia, would you take grapes from a stranger or indeed would you take grapes from a stranger then give them to another stranger? They had burst in my rucksack and seeped out and onto my hoodie. They were red grapes so it looked as if blood was seeping from me. When I first saw the stain I became alarmed, had I cut myself somehow? I laughed when I realised it was only grape juice. **I wore my HOPE hoodie constantly since I arrived in Paris.** This hoodie was my beacon of hope and it was staying with me. I only took it off when I went to bed or when it was too hot.

Suddenly Alicia transformed herself, her head and back straightened up and apart from her limp she began to walk as everyone else did, she even looked happy. She stopped at a shop selling clothes, there were a couple of portable trolleys outside the shop displaying lingerie, socks and tights. Alicia went into the shop had a look around, then came back out to look at the trollies that were filled with "on sale" garments, and then back into the shop. I was happy for her as this was normal. Indeed it reminded me of my daughter dragging me in and out of shops and then finally buying something from the first shop we went into.

I crossed over to the other side of the road, as she had been walking back and forth between all the shops on that street and I did not want her to notice me, certainly not now. So I observed from the other side of the street which also allowed me to see directly into the shops that she went into.

Alicia left the clothes shop without buying anything but went into a shoe shop two doors up and purchased a pair of boots. She then returned to the clothes shop.

Alicia purchased some items from that shop, I was surprised at both shop purchases for I thought maybe she did not have any money left as there was no food purchased during the day. She may have paid for these items by bank card, but I am not entirely sure.

As she was leaving the shop, Alicia lifted some items from the trollies outside and walked on. The lady in the shop saw her do this and ran out shouting on her, but Alicia did not hear and walked on.

I immediately ran out onto the road without looking trying to get to the shop assistant before she called for the police. Just as I stepped onto the road, I felt the force of two bikes hit me, the people on the bikes fell towards the road, but I managed to grab them from falling totally over and into the oncoming traffic. Luckily they had applied their brakes so the impact while sore was not that bad for all three of us. I apologised profusely while I continued to run across weaving in and out between the passing traffic.

I got to the other side and explained quickly that it was only two items she took, I paid the shopkeeper the money and she was ok with that.

Alicia then went into a mobile phone shop, and again I crossed over and observed from the other side of the road. Alicia talked to the phone assistant while smiling and laughing. After around 15 minutes a manger arrived at the desk with a phone, looked like a new iPhone. I though perhaps she had insurance on her old iPhone and this would be a replacement. Alicia looked normal and a typical happy nineteen year old teenager. I was happy for her but recognised that this was a temporary lapse from the reality that she had been previously in.

When Alicia met her mum and the police at the hostel, she managed to pull the wool over their eyes by acting as if she was a normal teenager and that "all" was ok. But that was further from the truth, and based on what they saw how could anyone dispute Alicia's mental health?

Earlier in the week I gave the police photographs and filed another missing person report (Thursday). But not one police officer noticed her as a missing person. The police officer who took my statement ensured me that her photograph would be instantly with every officer in Paris. At the time that gave me a sense of relief. I even emphasised the immediate police help to the family.

However, we passed several police officers and not one of them noticed or stopped Alicia, even despite her displaying signs of a person in distress. Afterwards in my research, I would discover the sheer number of missing people, how could the police know of everyone, how could they keep each one of those missing photographs in their heads. **The police need everyone's help in finding a missing person, they can't do this on their own.**

This situation further backed up my own internal feelings of not asking the police to become involved, indeed if I had stopped a police officer and told them, I don't think I would have been able to follow her anymore. And I would have lost her altogether to the streets of Paris. Plus the police definitely would not have become involved on a 3$^{rd}$ occasion. Therefore, I was content in my decision not to involve the police at the present moment. Her parents would soon be here and they could take over.

Back to the phone shop, Alicia gave the shop assistant her bank card, but it was handed back to her after it failed to process correctly. I could see that Alicia was disheartened when she left the phone shop without the new phone.

# 'Mass' and food

Shopping was now over and we walked through a narrow street. As we came to a park, Alicia stopped, and began to turn her head and looked all around, as if to see if she was going in the correct direction. This led me to believe that this is not the first time that Alicia had been in this neighbourhood. Alicia then turned around and began walking back towards the direction we just came from. After a couple of minutes she turned around and began walking in the original direction. In the meantime it was comical if you were to see my antics of jumping behind obstacles in an attempt to avoid being seen. It actually brought a smile to my face.

Our route took us through a narrow pathway and then onto a larger road in a busy neighbourhood. Within a few minutes Alicia arrived at a church that had mass starting soon. She looked at the signs outside and entered the church and was greeted by the priest with a smile, she sat about three rows from the front.

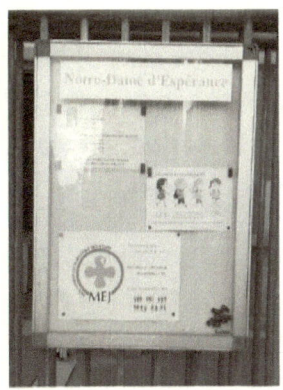

I approached the priest who was standing at the door. I explained to him what was happening and asked him if he knew Father Andre, but there are many priests in Paris and outlying districts and he could not recall that name.

I asked the priest could he give Alicia this money *(I handed money to him money to give to Alicia to buy food and drink)* because I now believed she had no money left. I explained that Alicia had not eaten or drank all day. He said he could not give her the money. But he said he will invite her to a special mass on Sunday (tomorrow) and he will see what he can do. I was taken aback, why could this priest not give her the money? I now felt that I was totally alone, two priests I asked for help and none came to the rescue. I truly needed their assistance, at this stage I needed anyone's assistance.

However, I was glad to be able to sit for an hour, I even got the chance to remove my shoes. I began to massage my sore and aching feet one at a time. This might have appeared to be a bit cheeky to do that in a place of worship, but my feet were in agony and goodness knows how long I would have to continue to follow Alicia. This reminded me of the days of my Christian upbringing and indeed when the humility and selfless love of Jesus when he washed the feet of his disciples at the Last Supper (John 13:1-15), this was the night before his Crucifixion. I thought to myself, if it was ok for Jesus, then it was sure ok for me to rub my feet.

I sat at the very back of the church, near the exit so wasn't noticeable by anyone. I was hoping that when Alicia left the church she would soon make her way to wherever she was going to stay for the night.

The priest walked around the congregation and handled his microphone to anyone who wanted to speak (it was all in French). To my surprise Alicia took the microphone and in English said, **"God is good and God is great, love and peace to everyone."** Alicia sat down with a smile on her face. Tears streamed down my face as I watched and listened to her, she was happy and smiling. For another brief moment in our day's journey the horrific torture that Alicia was enduring had been released for a momentary lapse of time in this French church.

Just before the end of the service, some young teenagers came in with buns, cakes and some other food. My spirts lifted as I thought that the priest had arranged this for Alicia, maybe he did or perhaps this was a weekly event, I don't know? Certainly the people that attended this church seemed to be from a poorer neighbourhood? Alicia went to the toilet in the church as all the other parishioners began to leave, and quite a lot stopped at the tables and began to take all the food and drink. I thought 'Sweet Jesus' leave some for her. Alicia took a long time coming out from the toilet. I got worried and asked if there was a back entrance from the toilets, luckily there was not.

Alicia finally appeared and made her way to the exit, by this time there was only a couple of items left for eating. She stopped at the table and asked the girls how much money did they cost? You could see that indeed Alicia was hungry. They said no it's ok, it's free! But Alicia was having none of it, she took her last coins from her pocket and gave them to the girls, she kept around 1 euro 50 cents, as far as I could see.

She took the bun and left the church with a smile that made her beautiful and happy face glow.

But that did not last long, it was now nightfall and Alicia was hobbling along with her several bags in tow. She stopped and put the items into one bag and discarded the empty bags. By now Alicia was walking at a snail's pace, the pain in her feet must have been unbearable.

Alicia stopped at an ice cream shop and went in and she asked what the price for a cone was. Alicia rumbled around her pockets and finally pulled out a few cents that she had left. I tried to get their attention by waving and beckoning that I would pay, but it was too late she had turned to leave the shop.

Her head and stance was now back to the bend downwards position. I felt her pain as she walked with tears streaming from her eyes. A sight that I was well used to, but one that was so extremely painstaking to accept.

The same routine as before continued, Alicia when finding some light would stop and write in her diary, I could hardly bare to watch her, and I cried along with her.

When Jesus carried the cross he was physically and emotionally suffering. In Alicia's case her cross was her diary, religious book and her plight to save her family.

I wanted to take her in my arms and shield her from the pain that was inflicting her. I wanted to fight the demons that were putting her through these negative connotations of trauma and torture. But I felt hopeless, I even felt that her Christian priests had abandoned her. I knew if I approached her, she would quickly come out of her nightmare and back into the reality were she would convince anyone of being a happy teenager.

And many times throughout the day I considered awakening her as an option to reduce her living hell. But if I did then there was a huge possibility that I would lose her from my sight forever, and that was definitely not an option that I could bare or indeed wanted.

# Knocked Down by a Car

It was dark, nightfall had arrived. We walked around the busy streets and I hoped that she would start to go back to her hostel. Wherever that was?

People would stop and turn around to stare at this teenager hobbling along with tears falling from her eyes. Only a couple of people actually stopped and asked her if she was ok, she nodded and walked on, as did the people who asked her.

[When Alicia left the phone shop. She was walking along the pathway, I was around twenty or so feet behind her. A lady and a man turned around looked at Alicia and then ran back towards her. Alicia's passport was hanging out of her rucksack, (I did not even notice that) the lady pushed it back inside the rucksack pocket. Alicia smiled and said thanks. There are some genuine good people out there.]

We came to a busy street and a pedestrian crossing, McDonalds was on the corner situated to the right of us at Place Léon Blum, As usual I went quickly up and became parallel with Alicia, making sure I was standing to her left side.

As I looked at Alicia I saw her make a forward movement without waiting for the lights to change, she walked onto the road. However, I jumped out first, a car slammed on its breaks but it hit me with enough force to send me flying forwards and into Alicia. Luckily neither of us were hurt. I ended up with a bruise on my leg but apart from that all was ok.

As I bumped into Alicia, I think I said,

"Jesus that was lucky, what a coincidence meeting you again Alicia".

I tried to speak with her but she kept walking back towards the street that we had just left. I caught up with her and said,

"Alicia I'm starving, do you not want something to eat from McDonalds with me?"

Alicia at first said "no", and carried on walking, I asked her again and she said "ok, but I'm a vegetarian".

I replied "ok we can find somewhere else to eat".

"No it's ok, I can get a salad". I told her that I think that they do vegetarian burgers here. But unfortunately they no longer served them.

I stood in line waiting to get served while Alicia went to the toilet upstairs and to get a seat. It took ages to get served and I was becoming concerned in case Alicia left without me noticing.

I got upstairs with our food, and Alicia's behaviour had now changed back to that of a chatty teenager that I once remembered. We talked about our families, friends and whatever came to her mind. I told her that her dad and Alma had come over to look for her. She said "yes, I have been thinking about my dad, did you see him?"

I told her "no, I never got a chance to meet them as they were with Father Andre". I told Alicia that Father Andre had a place for her to stay and a job and would she like to go and see him?

"No" she replied, I don't think he liked me, I got that feeling when I met him, and no I don't want to go meet him again."

I was taken back by what Alicia had said and I was glad that I did not stop her earlier to ask her to go to Father Andre's church.

We also talked about Sofia and the kids and how she hasn't seen them that much due to being at University and other typical teenager stuff in her life.

But yet, I could see and sense that this was a fabricated wall of deception that Alicia was putting up. A false wall that she had built to entertain those that knew her and to keep the pain of what she was currently experiencing hid.

I explained to Alicia that her family were worried about her and I was not in Paris by chance but rather to find her and make sure she was ok. I asked her to forgive me for lying about being in Paris on business. Alicia was ok with that, she smiled and told me it's ok and that I don't have to worry about her.

Alicia's displayed different mood emotions, the first one I experienced was when I first found her in Paris. Her mood was in-between happiness and sadness. The second mood swing was while I followed her and that was of extreme unhappiness and physical pain to which Alicia was clearly suffering, this was maintained for the majority of the time. The other mood was of a sad happiness and that appeared when I spoke with her at McDonalds and also witnessed when she went shopping.

I was concerned how this meeting was going to end. Alicia now aware that I was following her would not want me to continue to follow. What was I going to do if she insisted that I stayed away? I knew deep inside that no matter what Alicia wanted, I could not morally stop following her. Alicia's safety had to come first over all else. It would have been reckless if I had walked away and left her to wander around Paris in her state of mind.

I was in Paris to locate Alicia, I did that, and now I had to keep Alicia in view, and safe until her family arrived in Paris.

I asked Alicia, if there was anything that she needs? At first she said no, and then, "Well, there is one thing you could do, can you find me a place to sleep tonight?" Alicia had nowhere to go, if it wasn't for me getting knocked over, we would have been wandering the streets all night.

# No room at the Inn tonight

I got out my phone and started looking for a place for Alicia to stay on the internet, but there was no availability in Paris. This was possibly due to the 48th Ryder cup matches. I was struggling to find any hostels or hotels with availability. I could see that Alicia was becoming irritable and wanted to leave. I told her that she could have my bed (my hostel was also full), but she didn't want to stay in a room with three other men, which was understandable. (It was a mixed dorm of four beds, but it was still three other men staying in the room).

Alicia now had enough of waiting around, she became fidgety and couldn't sit any longer and decided to get up and leave, and she was beginning to go back into her other state of mind.

She said "its ok, God will provide" and walked off. I hurried to keep up with her, I walked a short distance behind while I continued to search for accommodation on my phone. Alicia now knew I was following her. I ran up and told her that her Mum and Antonio was searching for a hotel for her, and that they will get one soon, but she walked on while saying "it's ok, I don't need one now, you can leave me alone, God will provide."

I continued to walk behind Alicia while searching on my phone for a hotel. Back in home Antonio was also trying to find a room for the night.

The streets were now getting busy, so I had to stop searching and left that to the parents to do. My main concern was concentrating on keeping Alicia in my sights.

It was getting colder and I was beginning to feel the chill of the night. I left my coat back in my hostel as day times were too hot plus it was one less thing to carry. And at night my routine was to return to get my coat and start the night leg of my searching.

Alicia never looked around once to see if I was still there. She was in agony with her feet and was still carrying her bag of shopping. I mentioned earlier that I could walk with her and carry them for her, but she had insisted that I now left her alone.

After another hour of walking, Antonio phoned and said that they have managed to get a room in a hostel for her. They texted the address over to me. It was further away from our location, and we needed to get a taxi. I hobbled up to Alicia and told her that her mum and Antonio have found a hostel for her. At first it took a bit of convincing to finally get her to say yes.

We arrived at the hostel, went to check in, disaster struck, the room was not booked for tonight, they had made a mistake and it was booked for the following night. Plus to add to our misery they were fully booked. The receptionist pointed us in the direction of two other hotels close by. I managed to persuade Alicia to come with me to check those out. But they too were full. Again Alicia had enough, "God will provide" and off she went again, while saying, "I'm ok, I want to be left alone, you don't need to follow me, go back to your hostel."

This reminded me of the bible story and the frustration of a mother and father looking for a room for the night to give birth to their baby Jesus. It also typifies society that even in present day people can turn a blind eye to those in desperate need of food or a roof over their heads. And so far that's all I have experienced from the priests of Paris city, when I actually needed their help none was provided.

I followed as usual, this time keeping a further distance between us. However, this neighbourhood was different, it gave me concerns, and it was not your normal city street. It was dark and not well lit, nor where there many people around, easier for a person to be bungled into a vehicle and taken without anyone noticing anything.

Alicia was in great pain with her feet, walking even slower with her head still bend downwards towards the ground. In her state of being she would have been easy prey for... it's not even bearable to think what could possibly happen to a person in this state of mind or physical ability. Yet newspapers are filled with stories of children and adults gone missing or abducted.

She approached a bridge that crossed a canal. You had to walk up many stairs to cross this bridge. I waited until she was halfway across before I began to climb the stairs. When I got up to the top, I had lost her, I couldn't see her anywhere. I found the energy to run across the bridge and down the stairs, Alicia was nowhere to be seen. I began to panic, there were several small groups of people hanging around, sitting there talking and I could smell the weed as I passed them. It was pitch dark with subdued lights scattered around. It was extremely difficult to make out faces of people. I had contact lenses in my eyes and those did not function at their best in darkness.

I ran up the side of the canal, she was nowhere to be seen. I turned around and thankfully as I did I spotted her going behind three large bins. At first I thought perhaps she needed to go to the toilet, but when she came out behind them she had changed her clothes and boots. She went to one of the bins (which was a clothes recycle bin) and put all her old clothes and boots into it. Now she had no bag to carry apart from the rucksack on her back.

We continued to walk for another hour, Alicia was crying with the pain in her feet (probably more so from the newness of these boots), again the despair of helplessness at not being able to help her consumed me. I kept my distance and continued to follow.

Antonio phoned, and fantastic news they had found a hotel but there was only one room. But that was no problem because there was no way I was going to sleep and let her slip away in the morning unnoticed. I had intended in any event to stay in the lobby and keep diligent, so there was no need for another expensive room for me.

I ran up to Alicia excitedly and told her that Antonio had found another hotel for her. Alicia dismissed it immediately and told me to leave. I tried to persuade her but she was having nothing of it. I was forced to fall back and follow her again. I phoned Laura and Antonio and told them the bad news, but also that I will still try and convince her to go there.

We were walking up a street with a steep incline, Alicia turned left or at least I thought she had turned left on to another street. When I got to the corner she was nowhere to be seen. There was a small bar on the corner, so I went in to look, but there were only three people sat drinking and Alicia was not one of them. I ran around the corner, I couldn't see her anywhere, I ran up the other street but still no sign. I thought the worst, did someone pull up in a car and take her? Frantically I ran back into the bar, my whole body was shaking and my eyes filled with tears. I showed them a photo of Alicia and they smiled while holding my shoulder and told me not to worry, that girl is in their toilet. With a sigh of relieve I slumped onto a seat. Ten more minutes past and still no sign of Alicia. I was getting concerned so I asked them to check, sure enough she was still there. Alicia was sitting on a seat in the toilet lobby waiting area and getting some rest.

Soon afterwards she left and I followed. We began to walk downhill along a street not lit to well, there were buildings on one side and a park with a high fence on the other side. I kept close behind her.

I badly needed to go to the toilet. I should have went to the toilet when in the bar, but I didn't want to take the chance of her leaving unnoticed. Now my needs were desperate and there was nowhere to go. So I stood next to one of the small trees planted down the length of the street and 'watered the plants.'

By the time I had finished Alicia had crossed the road and was a bit further away than what I would have liked. A car drove past me as I walked away from the lanky tree that did nothing to hide me. The car slowly followed Alicia. A guy hung out the window and began to talk to Alicia, she kept walking with her head held downwards waving her hands for them to leave her alone. But the car continued to follow her. Then the car stopped and another person opened the back door and got out, the other man was still hanging out of the window and calling to her. By this time I was running down the street, shouting and screaming at the top of my voice. The guy looked around, ran back and jumped into the car, slamming the door shut as it sped off.

That was the final straw, I had enough of this playing nice. I approached Alicia and again I tried to convince her to go to the hotel. She was adamant that she was not going. I made it crystal clear that I was not going anywhere and I was definitely not leaving her side.

We continued to walk, Alicia still in pain and crying, both of us walked together in tears. I felt the blood of hopelessness flow through my veins, here I was at last and standing next to Alicia and I still couldn't remove the torture that consumed her.

Every so often, I would plead with Alicia to go to the hotel, but she always answered no, "God will provide."

I told her "God is providing, look he brought me here to you and you've got a place to stay for tonight. God has provided for you." But still she would not go to the hotel.

We arrived back into a busy well-lit area. There was a church or mission in front of us. Alicia entered the building, and I accompanied her.

There was some type of event or party still going on and it was packed with all black people. *[I'm by no way inferring any racial comment here. I was just outlining the situation that this world has forced upon us. Here are two white dudes going into an all-black private party in a religious place of worship with two rucksacks on their backs. What do you think? We were not challenged once by anyone. Every person on this earth is equal regardless of skin colour or faith.]* Alicia asked where the toilet was and went in. I stood there for a few minutes then left to go and sit outside on a stone bench in the freezing cold.

People started to leave the building, but no sign of Alicia, around twenty minutes later still no Alicia. I asked one of the partygoers who was leaving if there were any other exits? Afterwards I laughed into myself and thought "I actually asked if there was any other way out, wow" I went back into the Church to check that Alicia was ok. She was sitting at a table just outside the toilets with her head leaning on her hands and sleeping. A lady came over and shook her saying the church was closing now and that she had to leave. I was so thankful to the people in this church for allowing a stranger to come in and rest, their unknown hospitality was kindness, a thing that the world today needs to gain more of.

We left the building and proceeded to walk, Alicia was becoming very weary. So I explained to her that: "I had to stay by her side, and what would her family say if I left her here in the middle of the night, on her own and something happened to her? I couldn't bear to live with that, never mind what your family would think. Plus it's freezing out here, you need to go and get some rest for the night. Then I can get back to my own hostel."

I pleaded with Alicia to go to the hotel and get a good night's rest for all her walking tomorrow.

Alicia finally agreed and after around 30 minutes of waiting for a taxi one finally arrived. I got Alicia checked in at the hotel. The clerk at the desk had been updated by Antonio, so he knew what was happening.

Alicia went to her room, which was around the corner from the reception desk on the ground floor. I asked the desk clerk if it would be ok to stay in the lobby of the hotel. *[I felt terrible that I had lied to Alicia, however there was no way I was leaving her alone. After all I still had to keep her safe for her family arriving on today. (It was now around 2 am)]*

The clerk said sorry but I can't allow you to stay in the lobby. I asked to use the toilet and I spent the next 15 minutes in there heating up before I went out to stand across the road in the freezing cold dark night without a coat, but it had to be done.

When I came out of the toilet, the man said, "That's a double room that has been paid for, so I'm sure since you are a guest you can sit in the lobby," as long as you don't fall asleep and snore. I laughed into myself, because back home I'm always getting a nudge or a kick to stop me snoring. I went into the small reception area and sat there watching some YouTube videos on my laptop to keep me awake. I wanted to sleep, but I couldn't take the chance in case Alicia decided to leave.

Morning came and the duty manager gave me one of the freshly baked croissants that had just arrived together with a coffee. I left the hotel at around 7.30 am and went outside to stand. I did not want Alicia to see me sitting there as I had agreed that I would be staying at my own hostel and then flying home that morning. I left a letter and money in an envelope for the changeover clerk to give to Alicia when she went for breakfast.

I wanted Alicia to be able to buy food and drink until her parents arrived (today) around 6 pm on Sunday the 30$^{th}$ of September.

I went outside and stood across the road, it was freezing. So I ended going back into the hotel for a heat then back out again. I walked up and down the street to keep warm while still ensuring I kept an eye out for Alicia leaving.

I passed a self-serve laundry half way up the street and it was open. So I went back to the hotel and asked the clerk to phone me when she was leaving the hotel. I then went back up and sat in the laundromat. After around 30 minutes I got the phone call that Alicia was leaving, I asked if she got the letter, the clerk said yes but she left it on the table, saying she did not want to open it.

Alicia passed the window of the laundromat, I came out and ran as fast as I could back down to the hotel to get the letter. As I ran my leg gave way to excruciating pain, I fell to the ground and landed on my side, rolling over onto my back. As I rolled the momentum got me back up onto my feet, I tried to run but I had to drag my right leg behind me. The pain was unbearable. I got to the hotel, and picked up the letter while saying to myself, 'I'm a stupid bastard I should have left the letter there.'

Alicia was getting near to the top of this long street.

As I ran, dragging my leg behind me, strangely it began to get better, though I was still limping quite considerably. Thankfully, Alicia was still limping a bit to, though not as much as the day before.

# My Anguish

As I followed Alicia it was again apparent she was still experiencing mental health issues. I followed Alicia along a busy road with a market at the side of the path, the sun had risen and it was getting quite hot. Alicia did her usual stops and blessed some items, while writing in her diary. Alicia would cry and my tears would follow suite, it became our unknown joint ritual, a painful bond of togetherness in a plight that was slowly destroying the fabric of her young life.

It was around twenty seven hours since I last slept. And I had very little sleep since arriving in Paris. Physically I had become totally drained, and mentally I was desperately trying to hold on to my mental faculties.

At around 10 am we came to an extremely busy area with people and traffic totally surrounding us. Alicia stopped walking and as I stood at the doorway of a shop the pain in my leg was horrendous and was hampering my ability to walk. I asked the shopkeeper for some pain killers. They brought them to me and while I was paying Alicia began to move again. I hobbled to keep up, but the pain was holding me back and making it extremely difficult to walk and to keep up with her.

Several roads were now going off in all different directions. A busy hotel with many buses outside was on the opposite side of the road. Another road led to a bus station. Another road took a long curve towards a subway station. Another road went straight ahead and the last one went back towards where we had just come from. Most were wide roads with lots of buses and cars travelling in every direction, hundreds of people walked along the payments.

One moment Alicia was right there in front of me. And the next she was gone, in a split second she had vanished before my eyes. It was similar to sitting in front of a magic show and the magician making the person on the chair next to you vanish into thin air.

I was frantic, there was too many people all around me now, and every one of them was blocking any clear view and hampering my movement. I hobbled backwards and fro from street to street, showing people her photo and trying to describe what she was wearing. I went inside the hotel just in case she had went to use their toilet, but she wasn't there, Alicia was nowhere to be found.

Since following her I had a few scary times when I thought I had lost her. But now this time I had really lost Alicia. I could not comprehend what had just happened.

How could I be that stupid?

How the fuck could I have lost her?

Why did I fail her now, why the fuck!?

Jesus Christ in heaven above, Why…Why…Why…Why?

Even today when I read or recall this part of my story tears are streaming from my eyes, the emotions that I experienced at that time are still as powerful as they were then.

When I realised that Alicia was not going to be found, I finally made the most unbearable call to her mum. They were already travelling towards the airport. Now instead of coming to get their daughter they were coming to search for a daughter who had a mental health issue.

Antonio called me back and asked me to report the current situation to the police as he was advised by the foreign office to do. I did, but it wasted around 50 minutes of search time. After a few phone calls and finally getting someone in the French police who could translate our conversation, the result was negative. They could not help us, regardless of what I said on the mental health of Alicia.

After the call I hired a taxi to patrol the streets with me, finally after over an hour of searching by taxi, I asked the driver to stop at the Arc De Triomphe.

As I left the taxi I slumped to the ground in utter despair, crying uncontrollably as I looked around at the many roads and thousands of people in my view. How could I possibly find her in this city again? It's impossible. My adrenaline rush had stopped and I was entering a state of a nervous breakdown. Now that I knew I wasn't finding Alicia I had lost all of my hope. The time to have my mental breakdown was now. They say real men don't cry, but fuck that, real men do cry, and man I wasn't holding anything back.

The Signs that I began to display were the pathway towards hell. I had chest pains, difficulty breathing, I was trembling, I had dizziness, I felt sick to my stomach, and my mood swing went from looking for Alicia in the crowds of passing people to where I stood and then crumbling to the ground in despair.

Hope had almost vanished. Without hope I had nothing. I kept saying over and over in my head, "how could I have lost her, how?" The pain and the beating up of myself was becoming unbearable. And when I did settle down, I imagined the worst of things, what about Alicia? I have let her down, what if she walks out in front of a car? What if someone abducts her? My mind filled me with hundreds of "What If" scenarios, my mind in a negative downhill spiral to the point of no return. Darkness and despair began to control me. I even had suicidal thoughts in my head while thinking if anything happens to Alicia, it will be my fault.

I phoned home and spoke with Sofia, I had to speak with her, I had to pour out my heart yet I knew that she was suffering to. Yet she still listened to my screaming and crying, while she attempted to get me to calm down. I felt useless, and hopelessness had grown firm roots within my mentality and were spreading fast. My mental health was crumbling and falling into the abyss.

After talking with Sofia I began to calm down. I looked in every direction with tears streaming from my eyes, trying to find some sort of sign…anything. But there was no sign. By this time I could hardly see anyway, my eyes had totally puffed up as a result of my overwhelming emotions. Here I was on my own, I lost a teenager who possibly had a severe mental health issue. It would be my fault if anything happens to her.

How could I live with myself?

How could I face her parents when they arrived in Paris and without their daughter in my sights?

I wanted to find a stone and crawl underneath it. How could I have given everyone so much hope and then let them all down so badly?

What about my own family back in Spain, I had let them down, what would they think?

It was Alicia that I had let down the most, who was going to look out for her now?

# Losing Alicia and the New Search

I found my niece on the 5th day of continuous searching for her, I had roughly 2 to 3 hours sleep per day and had no sleep for the previous twenty seven hours. I lost her again on the 6th day as her parents were flying to Paris.

I stood at the side of one of the many roads near the 'Arc de Triomphe' in utter despair. Depression was only a fragment of what I was experiencing, God only knows what Alicia was feeling or going through. Roads were coming off this landmark in many different directions, there were thousands of people and cars travelling in all directions. I didn't know where to start looking or indeed did I have the strength to search again?

My only salvation was phoning home, Sofia tried to calm me and give me positive encouragement, only time would tell. Mentally Alicia was in a bad place and could have easily been abducted or knocked down by a vehicle. It would have been my fault as I was the one that found her and then lost her. How would I ever have forgiven myself?

I began to calm down and I began to remember my rainbow and subway sign, **"There is light at the end of the tunnel,"** though in this instance I couldn't fathom how I was going to see that light? I focused my mind to what tasks I had to do next. The seed of hope was not fully dead. Hope would only die the day I left Paris, and it would have been impossible for me to have left Paris now.

I slowly began to believe in **HOPE** again, and over the next few hours hope began to grow as a newly planted seed.

Around seven hours later and after searching the streets I met Laura, Antonio and Alma as they arrived in Paris city centre.

It was the worst feeling I have ever experienced. I had to look into their tearful eyes and say how sorry I was. Saying sorry was a total understatement to how I felt. Despite my new found hope I was still beating and torturing myself from the inside out.

Since I had little sleep they suggested I went back to my hostel to get some rest while they went to search. However, it didn't feel right to sleep, so I told them I was going to follow up on a 'sign' that popped into my head, a 'sign' that reminded me of a special mass that the priest had invited Alicia to attend at the church we attended yesterday. I thought, with some luck she will go to that mass.

The journey to the chapel took me around one hour of walking. I took several wrongs turns so it took longer to get there. I arrived at the church and walked up and down the packed aisles scanning to see if I could find her. But it turned out useless. She wasn't there.

On my return journey back to my hostel. I saw a girl in the distance. There were only a few people on this dimly lit street. This girl turned left at the end of the long street. Plus this person did not fully match the description of Alicia nor of Alicia's image stored in my mind. This girl wasn't limping at all. But yet there was something that made me run as fast as I could to the bottom of the street, chasing after this shadow of hope. At this stage I would have followed the devil to the pits of hell to find her.

It is surprising where you can get the strength to overcome your pain. I ran faster than what I thought I could have run, which was pretty fast considering my limp. As I reached the end of that road, this shadow turned left at the bottom, only this time I got less of a glimpse of her. I had no natural light as it was nightfall and only dim lights from streetlamps shown my way. I ran faster than before determined that I was not going to lose this person. I needed to get there quickly as it was a busier street with many hundreds of people and cars passing by. I put every seed of hope and faith that I had managed to retain into that person being Alicia. I had let my imagination run riot.

My gut and mind convinced me that it was Alicia, even although there was not a shred of evidence that pointed to that person being Alicia.

I got to the end of the road, it was busy with people and traffic moving around in every direction. I stood at the corner looking anxiously through the crowds on all sides of the streets. Finally my eyes landed on the person I had run to find, she was standing facing a bank machine.

My sign was indeed correct, I had found Alicia yet again from this needle in a haystack of a city. I could finally breathe once more.

# Second Miracle

I phoned Laura to let her know I had found Alicia, but no answer, I phoned Antonio but no answer either. I tried several other times but still no one answered their phones. I desperately needed help to keep her in my sights. I phoned Sofia to let her know that I had found Alicia and to ask if she could try to contact Laura and get her to phone me, Sofia was overjoyed. I was so glad that I could give her this positive news.

It really was another miracle, I managed to find her twice and both times it boiled down to a split second of timing and a change to my original plans.

Antonio now returned my call and I gave him the street I was now on and asked him to hurry. He called Laura. Luckily they were not too far away from me, they had been in a church and they thought I was only calling to say I was going for a sleep.

About ten minutes later Antonio ran up the street to where we were, Alicia was walking down that street in a brisk movement, her limp totally gone. Antonio stopped walking and stood directly in front of Alicia with his arms held outwards to try and stop her from passing him, but she pushed past. Laura and Alma arrived as she pushed passed Antonio. They too attempted to stop her. But she kept walking and pushing forward each time they tried to stop her. Alicia was determined that no one was going to stop her.

They desperately tried to talk with Alicia as they walked but she wasn't listening. Alicia turned right and into the entrance of an underground station, she walked down to the lower level. Laura finally had enough and blocked her from going any further. Alicia could no longer get passed and still she was adamant that she was not going anywhere with them and was staying here in Paris on her own.

Sofia had told Laura the night before she left for Paris that she needs to bring on that "Rottweiler" attitude that she normally has when in tough situations. She needs to be harsh with Alicia and not to let her walk all over her with false claims that she is ok. The proof was obvious, Alicia needed help and quickly.

Finally they managed to persuade Alicia to come with them and they went into a restaurant next to the subway station. In the meantime Antonio and I had been speaking with the

Spanish foreign office in Paris to keep them up to date and advise them that Alicia had been found. They suggested that Alicia should be taken to the Psychiatric hospital in Paris immediately. The hospital is also well known for its excellent help and treatment. But Laura was reluctant to have Alicia admitted to hospital that night.

Laura not only wanted to keep her daughter close to her for as long as possible, but she dreaded the thought of Alicia being taken from her yet again. I knew in my heart that this was the right decision for Laura to make.

Laura and Alma had convinced Alicia to come back and stay in their hotel for the night. As a family they needed this time to be together, this was a night of hope, and a time to be together, to talk, to hug and just to be there to laugh and crying with each other.

I left them all at the restaurant and as I walked back to my hostel, my body now craved food, something I had not properly felt since I had arrived in Paris. Food and rest had not been a priority for me, but now I needed to eat. I walked aimlessly around the streets of Paris looking for proper food and not just a quick bite. But it was late and most restaurants were now closed. And the ones that were open, well let's just say I did not really feel in the mood to sit in one alone. While I was walking I phoned Sofia to update her on all the developments, I had no opportunity to do this since I found Alicia. I finally found an Indian restaurant and ordered a Korma for takeaway. I took the food back to my hostel and ate it in the lobby of my hostel. I went to sleep content that Alicia was found and now in safe hands.

# Monday Morning – 1st October 2018

The next morning they decided that Alicia would be taken to the hospital for observation and Alicia willingly agreed, while saying, "But I'm leaving after they examine me." The family took her by taxi, but the taxi ended up at the incorrect address. This turned out to be a good thing, one of the top psychiatric doctors was giving a speech in the building that they had inadvertently arrived at. He came over to see Alicia and spoke to the family and he offered to assist them.

Shortly after being admitted to the Paris hospital, Alicia became distant from her family, and did not want to speak with anyone. However, on Sunday 6th October Alicia was described as getting better she was chatty and laughing while trying to make sense to what had happened to her.

The French hospital and Alicia's local hospital were arranging the best plan for Alicia. On the 10th of October she landed back home and was taken to the local hospital on her own accord. Alicia remained there for a few more weeks.

It was great for the family having her back home. Alicia left her local hospital with a prescription of medication and she continued to make outpatient visits.

Alicia is recovering and slowly getting her life back again. It is extremely sad how a young happy and outgoing teenager can suddenly be possessed and consumed by religious voices. Voices that demanded that she incur extreme pain in order to be worthy.

Alicia's believed that the voices inside her head came from the Virgin Mary. These voices made Alicia believe that with every blister she received in her tiny feet, a soul would be released into heaven. Alicia was enduring pain and suffering while believing that she was helping others less worthy of god's attention.

Later Alicia would explain that she did what she did because of the voices in her head. These voices told her that they would harm her family if she did not do what she was ordered to do.

Alicia will be the only one that can tell her story and what she actually experienced during her time in Paris. I have made assumptions to what I saw and subsequent heard from her family.

# Leaving Paris

On the Saturday I found Alicia we walked for over eighteen hours and covered around 22 miles of walking. Now it was my turn to make my last walk in Paris City. I left Paris blissful that I had found Alicia and that she was now with her family and on a pathway of recovery.

Laura, Antonio and Alma were now with Alicia in the hospital and I was alone at the airport with my emotions that had encompassed and shadowed me for the last seven days.

To heal, I now had time to deliberate about what had materialised that week. While waiting to board my flight my mind replayed each day and my emotions became so overwhelmed that I wept as I relived Alicia's pain and my journey. That pain was soon replaced with thoughts of happiness on finding her. I think it would have been harder to live with myself if I hadn't found Alicia that second time.

I offered my assistance to Laura before I left Paris, but was not sure what I could have done to help anyway, as the adrenaline in my body departed and I was now a mental and physical wreck. But it was time that the family were left alone to deal with the issues at hand and to get their daughter the help that she needed for her recovery.

I flew out of Paris still believing that my work was not yet complete. I felt a sense of loss within my soul, and I could still fell Alicia's pain in every thought I had.

I arrived at my home airport, got into the car and my mind now focussed on being with my family, holding and hugging them. My family had been my resilience for the complete journey of searching for Alicia. And I could not wait to be back with them.

While this was an extremely traumatic event for everyone, it was now over and the road of recovery for everyone became the new roadmap of hope for all the family.

Paris is a city known for Love, romance and history, and it finally yielded and gave back love to a family being reunited after such a traumatic event. In Alicia's case, history will be recorded as a blessing from the universe or a calling from God.

Despite the rollercoaster of my emotions, I departed Paris knowing that Alicia was now in safe hands.

For Alicia and her family the journey to recovery will be one hell of a ride. For Alicia's disappearance and mental health issue affected the family in ways that one cannot fully understand. What happened to Alicia is not her fault, but how a family copes with this will be a deciding factor on how well and quick Alicia and indeed the family will recover. Being there for each other in an understanding and loving way will help build their resilience against an unwanted adversity that they all endured.

A year and a half later Alicia is on the mend and indeed she now plays a role as an essential worker in the COVID-19 era. I still get emotional when I think of our Journey through the streets of Paris city, I still cry when my mind recalls the events of witnessing her internal torture and how useless and powerless I felt to take away that pain for her.

That morning I lost Alicia back to the streets of Paris will continue to haunt and remind me of a time of extreme pain. But now my tears and thoughts are of happiness, for Alicia's life has been given back to her.

I further believe that there will come a day when Alicia is ready and she too will be able to talk openly and freely about her experience. This could help Alicia on her own journey of self-discovery while helping other teenagers come to grips with any similar adversity that Alicia experienced. Until then we hope that Alicia will grow from strength to strength.

## Mario: By reliving and telling his story...

Mario has managed to help free his mind from his adversities from a traumatic journey. That was a roadmap to his internal healing. It helped him make sense of what had happened and how he could reflect and recover from it.

As the author of writing Mario's journey I'm proud that he allowed me to be the story teller and author for his journey. Indeed Mario followed my own template of writing to free yourself from adversity and that's why he chose me as author for his journey to find Alicia.

Herein ceases Mario's story and his journey towards helping find a missing teenager in Paris. And Mario is now part of a network that assists in helping to locate other missing people. This is a journey that Mario and I now share.

Mario was never made aware of Alicia's mental health diagnoses and as such no assumptions have been made while writing or researching this book. At no time did Mario or the author try to diagnose or clinically name what Alicia was enduring or suffering from.

This story represents Mario's journey and the story is from his viewpoint of what occurred while he searched Paris for Alicia. He cannot say what Alicia was experiencing, he can only speak about what he witnessed and how it affected him. He wanted his story to be told to help others in a similar situation, to let them know that they are not alone, and to help set his mind free from the pain that he endured on this journey of hope. What Alicia experienced on her journey is her story and one that only she can tell.

# RESOURCES and Further Reading

## Beyond this point is the Author's viewpoints

Everything beyond this point represents the author's viewpoint based on experience, education and research. This section is not part of Mario's journey or story nor is the author suggesting that Alicia in Mario's story has any of the mental health issues outlined in the resource section. While in some instances we could make an informed decision however, that would be unprofessional. As such the resource section is designed to help you develop an understanding of mental health issues and assistance in forming resilience, which is a huge aspect of my plan to help people with mental health issues using writing resilience techniques.

I further believe that writing can help set you free and can be one form of resilience from your adversities. Throughout my journey in life I would create poems or stories to free my mind from injustices that I heard or read about or to set me free from difficult times or adversities in my daily live that troubled me. As the author of this book I to have suffered from adversities in my life which has affected my mental health at times.

I'm currently writing a series of books on how to free yourself from adversity by using your favourite singer as a means of encouragement to get you writing. These books can be found at https://www.Storylyrics.com Music is a journey to your heart and soul. Music will try to define your feelings and emotions but you can choose only to listen to music that harnesses the greatness in you.

'HI' is an independent and impartial aid organisation working in situations of poverty and exclusion, conflict and disaster. They work alongside people with disabilities and vulnerable populations, taking action and bearing witness in order to respond to their essential needs, improve their living conditions and promote respect for their dignity and fundamental rights. These programmes or national associations are known as "Handicap International" or "Humanity & Inclusion", depending on the country.

Mario took the above photograph while searching for Alicia. This was one of the areas that Alicia and Mario passed after he had found her. They both walked along many of the streets that he had previously walked in his search for Alicia. It was similar to lost ships passing unknown to each other in the darkness of the night.

## Missing in France

Every country have their own missing people. However the missing are not only the responsibility of that country or the missing's families. It is the responsibility of humanity to assist in helping to find those that are missing.

The child's safety is of paramount concern and in these instances all cases of missing runaway children should be investigated. The authorities must listen to what the child has to say before they are returned to their home or care facility. In all events it can sometimes be difficult to separate a runaway from that of a person gone missing, however regardless, any missing person must be investigated with a due diligence and a matter of urgency.

The website https://www.missinginparis.com has links to websites that contain information of the missing throughout the world. Please make a transformation to your normal daily routines, this can be done by actively helping to look for a missing person. Regardless of where you reside, it will only take a few minutes of your time. Look at photographs of the missing and look at people on your daily travels and holidays. It's as simple as that.

You can make a difference, a simple change of mind could help find a missing person.

## A few minutes of your time, Is all the 'Missing' ask.

With the death of a loved one there is a process of grieving which will vary from family to family, based on religion, country or "group" beliefs. The five stages of grieving not in any order are, denial, anger, bargaining, depression and acceptance. After acceptance those affected can begin to move forward.

However, you can never move forward when a loved one goes missing...Hope is your only salvation...Hope keeps you alive to endure the pain from everyday life. Because everyday life transforms from normality to hell... Hope is your only salvation from the world within your horrific nightmares.

Friends and families of the missing have no closure until the day they are reunited with their loved one. The missing are in an unknown domain, their families need your support and assistance to find their loved one. The police and authorities cannot do this alone, they need every person to help. The more eyes looking for the missing the better chance of eventually finding them.

You may wonder what you can do, but pure and simple: **Actively look when you leave your home, actively look when shopping and on holidays.**

Go to missinginparis.com, it lists missing people from around the world. Scan through some photographs and details of missing children or adults. It will only take a few minutes of your time and you could possibly help find a missing person. Please don't turn a blind eye, it will only take you a few minutes, but you could make a lifetime of a difference for a missing person's family and friends.

It is no big effort to take a moment to look at some photographs of the missing before you go on your day's journey. Sign up to the European Alert scheme and be notified when a person goes missing in your area. Finding a person in the golden hours would help make all the difference. And the more people helping, the greater chance we have of finding that missing person.

So instead of just reading about the missing, trafficked, kidnapped or abducted actual put the paper down and get involved. Involvement can take the form of many activities, donation, registering to help, actively becoming aware who is missing in areas that you travel to, lobbying government and local authorities to increase awareness and assistance to stop these horrific networks from succeeding in the abuse of "anyone." It could be someone from your family.

Act now and make a difference, it will make you feel you have achieved a sense of accomplishment of goodness for one aspect of your life's journey.

Scan the QR code to gain valuable information on Mood disorders. The Canadian Mental Health Association outline this as, *"Moods are our emotions. They affect us every day. Sometimes we're sad, other times we're happy. We might even be sad and happy in the same day. But sometimes people's mood can get "stuck" on sad. Or the moods might change a lot or become extreme. When this happens, it affects our lives. And it might be caused by a group of mental illnesses called mood disorders."* Mood disorders can also be an aspect of depression, psychosis or anxiety. CBT is a known and helpful way of therapy to helping people with a Mood Disorder.

## Every parent's worst nightmare

Take a look at the following video and immense yourself into that video. What if your child went missing? How would you feel? This is only a fraction of a taste of what a family experiencing a missing person would endure.

While the CCTV footage in the beginning of the video is a re-enactment. The scenes of families brought back together are all too real.

**What would your life be like if it was someone you knew who went missing?**

# HOPE Poem & Breathing Exercise

If despair is what you feel, let HOPE restore your faith

If misery fills your mind, let HOPE set your mind free

If you have nothing left to give, let HOPE be your saviour

If you think there is no HOPE left, then HOPE has not departed you, but rather you have departed from HOPE.

When there is no solid proof, HOPE is what you need. HOPE will give you the strength to carry on.

## Breathing Exercise

If your mind is frantic, then breathe in deep while spelling in your mind 'H - O - P - E'. Hold your breath and spell 'H - O - P - E'. Release your breath slowly while spelling 'H - O – P - E'. Repeat at least four times. That may help ease you. It certainly will stop your mind from thinking negatively for a short period. Do this when whenever you need to free your mind from negative activity.

# MissingInParis.com

**O**n the journey of existence on earth, some people have to endure more pain and sorrow than others. Some people live in houses and some on its cold and unwelcoming streets. Some people live in freedom and equality where others are exploited and abused. Some live in families and some are stolen away. The missing will always be missing until people do something about it.

**You can make a difference by actively looking for a missing person** as you go about your day to day duties:

*https://www.missinginparis.com*

MissingInParis.com has links to missing people websites where you can look at missing children and adult's photographs, you never know you may just come across one. This site will be updated to include new links and information about the missing.

Please when you go on holiday take a look at the missing in that area, you never know you might just save a life.

# Leah Croucher Age 19

Leah disappeared on February 15th 2109 at age 19, in Milton Keynes, on her walk to work. She was last seen on Buzzacott Lane, Furzton, at about 8.15am wearing a black coat, skinny black jeans and Converse.

Leah's mum Claire made an emotional appeal and further said on the 22nd of February, 'Whatever it is that has caused you to run away, please let us help or fix it.'

On the 25th May 2019, Chief Inspector Neil Kentish. Made the following statement, "I would like to take this opportunity to remind people of Leah's appearance; she is white, slim, with below shoulder length brown hair and sometimes wears glasses...I still believe that someone, somewhere, has a vital piece of information which will help us to find Leah. If you have, and for whatever reason you haven't already come forward, I would urge you to think of Leah's family and contact the police."

The teenager's parents Claire and John Croucher said "each day getting up is the hardest thing they do... every day Leah is gone is heart-breaking she is our beautiful, wonderful daughter...but HOPE is what keeps them going."

Anyone with any information on Leah should contact police on 101 quoting Thames Valley Police reference 4319 004 9929. Alternatively, contact Crime stoppers anonymously on 0800 555 111 or through their online anonymous form at www.crimestoppers-uk.org. No personal details are taken, calls cannot be traced or recorded and you will not go to court.

## Hearing Voices, you are not alone

When you are, writing, studying or listening to music or talking with others either singularly or in a group, you may hear voices in your head. Most of these voices are internally justifying the conversation or processing the task that you are attending to or trying to make sense of, or reiterate it in a way that your mind will understand.

For example:

Who does she think she is?

It's all about her..."

Or "I wish I was like her..."

I have so much to do. "I need to make my list of things to do...here they are...."

These types of inner voices can be endless. You are rationalising your thoughts, but more importantly these inner voices don't control you. And here is the major variance between "good inner voices" and "unhealthy inner voices".

The above are normal voices, voices that you understand, voices that you know belong to you and not of another person.

There are many inner voices that you do not generally hear. For example: A dog barks, you don't say to yourself "a dog has barked." Your inner voice does that automatically through learned connections. That inner voice is silent or at least it appears silent. What your inner voice might do is respond to that action, "why is the dog barking?" Your response to that inner question again could be routed in past experiences. For example, "it could be a burglar, the dog never barks that late at night?" Perhaps when you were younger you experienced an unhealthy event or trauma, dog bite, armed robbery or one of many other situations. You can see that your past experiences can shape your thoughts, decisions and responses in later life.

Moreover, voices that are dysfunctional are voices that tell you to harm yourself or others. Voices that command you to do rituals that usually involves your suffering in order to free or help others in society, sometimes these voices are wrongly justified by taking the presence of a spiritual or Godly stance. This is what I call the "God Dilemma". These type of voices can lead you to harm yourself or others.

Why?

Well, for the majority of us we are born into a religion, we are brought up in that religion, we perhaps go to a single denomination religious school. Religion is groomed into our very fabric. Perhaps your parents or carers were extremely religious and thrust or forced their own believes onto you? After all that's what our parents were forced to believe since their birth.

Then, when things go wrong in our lives we look towards God and religion for assistance. In some cases we believe that we are no good and to purge our evilness we must suffer in order to help ourselves or others escape their torture. And being the Good Samaritan we must suffer to free those lost souls.

Mother Teresa admitted she heard voices in her head, but her voices did not involve harming herself or others. These voices told her to build homes for people to live in. Similarly for some other people, their inner voices have put them into the servitude of helping others in their community without harming others. Yet, others hear voices that condemn equality and put their faith and/or country as the almighty, and harm others as a result of these unhealthy voices.

The God Dilemma is not only for inner voices, it also represents the worldwide believe that each person's religion is better or indeed is the only true one. Hence, why inner voices believed to be from God or Gods disciples can have a detrimental effect on a person's mental health. These thoughts become more intensified and believable when that person has experienced adversity or trauma in their lives.

When one hears Godly voices in their head that empowers them to do good for others in true equality on earth without any harm to themselves or others, well... that indeed would be the voice of a worthy god.

To everyone that has experienced harming voices from God, understand one thing. No true God would want any person to suffer, No true God would command you to harm yourself or others, in a nutshell No true God would want or make you suffer at all.

Moreover, a statement that you must virtuously forget and trash into the recycle bin of your mind and then immediately empty that recycle bin, is the notion that "suffering" is a Godly thing. Inner voices that inform you to suffer are the voices of hell and are certainly not from any God or religion worthy of your worship.

The good news, it's not all doom and gloom. There is HOPE. Scan the QR codes below and listen to these stories of women who have experienced traumatic voices in their head. They have come back from the depths of their depressions, anxiety and the belief that they were once failures. They have managed to change their lives around for themselves with understanding and help from others who believed in them.

More importantly they have discovered the true meanings of the voices in their head and how these voices are a manifestation of adversity and trauma that has occurred in their lives. In some cases these inner voices could be a result of Adverse Childhood Experiences, or excessive stress with exams, or family and relationship problems.

[Important: Brains are still developing. It has been proven that neuron connections in the brain will continue to be formed up to the age of 25+. Therefore, trauma, adversities and Toxic Stress can damage your child's neurobiological development. The solution is to work as a community to alleviate this risk as much as possible.]

Understand your unhealthy voices, allow them to be present, but give them no importance, let them pass through your mind, acknowledge them when they arrive, and allow them to depart without giving them any credence. [To do this read the resilience section of my book]

Understanding your inner voices can help you uncover why they are there. Are the voices re-enacting what you have experienced during an adverse event in your childhood?

This Ted Talk, titled "The Voices in my Head" is an emotional and uplifting story by Eleanor Longden who underwent dramatic changes in her life due to destructive Inner Voices. Eleanor was your typical student then one day she woke up as a different person. What happened to her?

In her story you will learn how eventually after a few years Eleanor went on and became top in her university degree and mastered in Psychology. She also outlines in certain circumstances that the wrong type of psychiatric help can be further detrimental to oneself. This 14 minute long video is uplifting to the core. It outlines **Hope and Resilience**, and that each of us can have the ability to mend ourselves. Scan the QR Code below to hear her story.

## The voices in my head, Eleanor Longden

*T*o all appearances, Eleanor Longden was just like every other student, heading to college full of promise and without a care in the world. That was until the voices in her head started talking... these internal narrators became increasingly antagonistic and dictatorial, turning her life into a living nightmare. Diagnosed with schizophrenia, hospitalized, drugged, Longden was discarded by a system that didn't know how to help her. Longden tells the moving tale of her years-long journey back to mental health, and makes the case that it was through learning to listen to her voices that she was able to survive.

# Hearing Voices
## An Insider's Guide to Auditory Hallucinations
## Debra Lampshire

*D*ebra's story of living with voices is a journey into the soul. Describing her experiences, we start to understand, and are able to better support those human beings living with loud heads. Debra is project manager for the Psychological Interventions for Enduring Mental Illness Project at the Auckland District Health Board (ADHB). In this unique and innovative position Debra works in the clinical setting leading the development of psychological strategies for positive symptoms of psychosis and the first non-clinician to do so. She is also a senior tutor with the Centre for Mental Health Research and Policy Development at the University of Auckland. This talk was given at a TEDx event using the TED conference format but independently organized by a local community.

# What the Voices in My Head Say
## Schizophrenia & Mental Illness

Around 1 in 10 adults hear voices in their heads as a result of one of a number of mental illnesses, including Schizophrenia. The Voices in My Head is a ground breaking documentary taking viewers in to their world, following the lives of 3 voice hearers through a hybrid of observational documentary and audio reconstruction.

# Hearing voices and hallucinations
## Juno's Story

*J*uno first starting having hallucinations when he was 14 and still at school. This meant he had to take his GCSEs while still in hospital. In this video he talks about what it was like for people to be scared of him because of his mental health, why he stopped taking antipsychotics and how having schizophrenia affects his everyday life.

# Lost In Reality
## Hearing Voices | Adrianne Roberts | TEDxChilliwack

*T*hree years ago she believed she was specifically selected by God to hear voices and sense presences, which were able to talk to her. She thought it was a gift. She started hallucinating scenarios and different environments that no one else could see or were apart. A straight forward woman who has experienced some unusual things. She shares her insight and thoughts regarding mental health from a unique perspective.

# Hearing Voices Network

This website has many resources to help you with hearing voices for children and adults.

Since the start of the Hearing Voices Movement back in the 1980s, we have amassed a wealth of information resources that available for free on the internet. Some of these will be downloadable from this site. Others will be linked to form this site.

# Hearing voices

Hearing voices is a common symptom of a mental illness, but not everyone that hears voices are unwell. This factsheet looks at what it can be like to hear voices, why you might hear voices and how to deal with them.

- Around one in 10 of us hear voices.
- Another term for hearing voices is auditory hallucinations.
- Hearing voices can sometimes be positive.
- Sometimes these voices can be negative and upsetting.
- Research shows that hearing voices is not always a sign of mental illness.
- Treatments for distressing voices can include medication, talking therapies and peer support.

This factsheet covers:

1. What does the term 'hearing voices' mean?
2. What is it like to hear voices and how is this condition diagnosed?
3. What are the different types of voices experienced?
4. What causes someone to hear voices?
5. How are they treated?
6. What treatment should the NHS offer me?
7. What if I am not happy with my treatment?
8. What are self care and management skills?
9. What risks and complications can voices cause?
10. Information for carers, friends and relatives

**How to**
cope with hearing voices

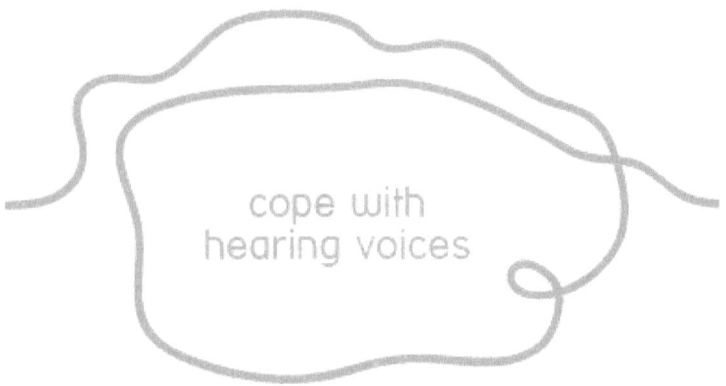

how to

cope with
hearing voices

# Coping Strategies for Hearing voices
**Extract from:** https://www.mentalhealth.org.uk

**Seek explanations to account for your voices:** Understanding where the voices come from and why, and what triggers them can be helpful in developing a coping strategy. Unless some meaning is attributed to the voices, it is difficult to establish a relationship with them in order to feel more in control. Approaches that discourage voice hearers from seeking mastery of the voices tend to yield the least positive results.

**Accept that the voices belong to you:** This is the essential first step in the process of developing your own point of view and taking responsibility for yourself. This is one of the most important and difficult steps to take.

**Discuss your voices:** This helps you learn to recognise their games and tricks, as well as their good aspects, and to identify patterns that are specific to given situations. This can help you to be better prepared for future onset of voices. Voice hearers may think they are alone in hearing voices. This can lead to feelings of shame or the fear of going mad. Anxiety often leads to the avoidance of situations that might trigger the voices, stopping people leading a full and rewarding life. Anxiety severely restricts freedom of movement, and strategies of avoidance often seem to exacerbate the problem.

# Manchester NHS

**Do you ever hear things that other people cannot hear? Are you worried about it?**

## What is it?

Although hearing voices is often associated with mental health problems such as psychosis or schizophrenia, there is lots of evidence that people without mental health difficulties also hear voices. Others worry that hearing voices means they are weird which often makes them feel more anxious and worried.

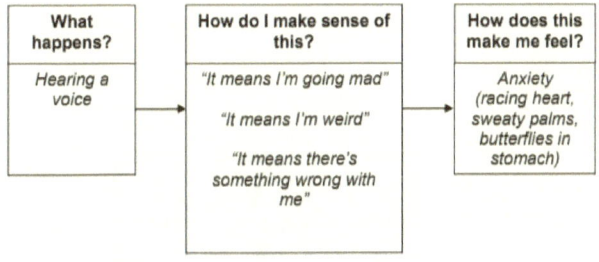

# Psychosis Research

"We are pleased to announce that we have launched an e-learning resource for cognitive behavioural therapies (CBT) for psychosis in collaboration with Health Education England, Greater Manchester Mental Health NHS Foundation Trust, and the University of Manchester. The resource provides training materials and role-play videos to enhance training in the formulation-based approach to CBT that we have been developing for over twenty years."

http://www.psychosisresearch.com/

Another helpful mental health resource website is, re Think Mental Health is found at https://www.rethink.org/ "We improve the lives of people severely affected by mental illness through our network of local groups and services, expert information and successful campaigning. Our goal is to make sure everyone affected by severe mental illness has a good quality of life."

# The God Dilemma

If you were to help an Alcoholic, would you give them alcohol to drink? Would you encourage them to drink?

**No you would not, their health should come first.**

If you were to help a drug addict, would you keep giving them drugs?

**No you would not, for their health should come first, and you would seek help.**

Yet people who have heard detrimental and hurtful voices from God or indeed any other religious voices, are sometimes still immersed into religion.

So if a person is displaying an overburden of unhealthy religious feelings, why would you continue to make religion an important aspect of that persons healing? The links below discuss religion and the hearing of voices.

https://livingwithschizophreniauk.org/religious-spiritual-delusions-schizophrenia/

*"The history of the world's major religions makes it clear that saints, sages, prophets, and teachers (such as Moses, Mohammed, and Teresa of Avila) have relied heavily on the inner voice as their inspiration, their guidance, and their authority."* **(Heery, 1989, p.75)**

The following is an extract from Premier Christianity, *"Another controversy is that it is common for people who experience psychosis to be given deliverance ministry – sometimes without their consent."*

And herein lays the God Dilemma. No true God would ask that of their child to suffer.

The God Dilemma is created when a person is still continually drawn to religion as a means to try and cure their dysfunctional inner religious voices. Whereas that person should be taking a break from religion in order to see the truth of the reality that they are now living in.

The God dilemma is what you face when you know you have been affected by an unhealthy dose of religion. A religion that has taken over your mind and reality, yet you are still forced to attend religion either by those inner voices or by others who believe that their god will cure you.

The God Dilemma is anything that is detrimental to your or others wellbeing, and knowing that you should probably be taking a break, but your faith and its followers tell you otherwise. And the guilt of taking a sabbatical could make your mental health deteriorate more, it's a catch 22 situation.

I believe the God Dilemma is a problem that needs a solution away from religion regardless of what faith that may be. **And only then can you possibly return to your faith and to your God with a renewed excitement for what you believe in.**

# Mental Health Issues

While this book originally began as Mario's story of searching for a missing teenager in Paris. It soon became 'one' with the author's concept of helping to highlight mental health awareness while providing resources to help people form a level of resilience with their issues.

The writing gave mental relief to Mario, and as he reminisced his journey in Paris with myself it helped set his mind free. As such if you cannot write about your journey yourself then you can talk about it and get someone else to write it for you. For some people it could just talking about their adversity with a friend, family member of counselling practitioner. These are some of the many techniques of resilience that can help you to recover from your adversities.

We cannot turn a blind eye to the Mental Health issues that have created a runaway situation for many children. Especially children in care, a higher percentage of children in care will run away at some point in their residence, either once or several times. Children in these situations can become extremely vulnerable and susceptible to slavery, human trafficking and abuse. Indeed any child or vulnerable adult is at the same risk in a missing person's incident.

Celebrities are now coming forward and making their mental health issues known. This in its own right is assisting in breaking the stigma and the old tradition of not talking about such things outside of the home or family. Now it's bang right out there in the open, where it should be. Workplaces are becoming more aware and by law businesses are becoming more of an informed and concerned workplace towards employees with mental health issues.

It's fantastic to see programmes of wellbeing being introduced into many workplaces, like mindfulness, meditation, healthy eating and exercise. All of these resilient techniques are proven to help reduce stress and depression.

*Ruby Wax is a loud, funny woman – who spent much of her comedy career battling depression in silence. Now her work blends mental health advocacy and laughs. [Extract from Ted Talks]*

We all sure do need a bit more humour in our lives. In this short video Ruby touches mental health head on, but in a funny and informative way. It reclassifies the stigma in people who suffer from depression and mental health issues. Today, more and more people are coming on board with the realisation that the brain is another organ that can suffer from health issues. There is nothing to be ashamed about. Mental health is like any other illness, if it needs treated then let's get on board and arrange the infrastructure to get people well again.

After all, if someone has a heart condition or cancer we look for cures. Mental health issues are present in almost every person. What separates one person displaying a mental health issue and another not, can be due to trauma, adversity, stress and toxic stress in their lives. However, some children are more adaptable and form resilience from their childhood trauma. It is further noted that a traumatised child who has one significant other present in their lives that they can turn to for advice and to be there for them will act as a major form of resilience for that child.

Furthermore, Ruby mentions in her video about how her mother would act in certain circumstances and this would inevitably pass mental health issues onto Ruby.

The positive point in all of this is knowing that childhood experiences can shape you for "better or worse." But they can also make you aware of why you are acting the way you are. And with this knowledge comes the ability to free yourself from the negative aspects of your upbringing and the understanding of your mental health and how you can adapt from adversity or trauma to lead a fulfilling and rewarding life.

Scan the QR code below to be enlightened and to have a laugh at a sad situation that can be turned around for the better.

# Ruby Wax on Mindfulness

L̲ECTURE @THE SCHOOL OF LIFE: *Ruby Wax argues that by better understanding better how our brains work, we can learn to rewire our thinking and find calm in a frenetic world. Wax seeks to help us start becoming more the master, and less the slave, of our own minds.*

# The one gift Santa can't deliver

This short video is reality for families in war torn countries where children are separated, missing or could even be trafficked. For God's sake these are children. Children that need the help of everyone, the world needs to develop a zero tolerance towards acts of racism, abuse and so forth.

*The only thing some children want this holiday season is to be reunited with their families. For nearly 150 years the International Committee of the Red Cross has worked to bring families and missing children separated by conflict or natural disaster back together again.*

# Humanity in Action

The ICRC and Red Cross help children and adults around the world. Without their help more children, women and men would be subjected to sexual abuse, trafficked or exploited. This short video explains some of what they do to help humanity.

*The ICRC works worldwide to protect the lives and dignity of victims of armed conflict and other situations of violence and to provide them with assistance*

# The right of an Adult to Disappear

Maëlys de Araujo at age 9 was reported missing on 27th August 2017 while attending a wedding with her parents. Nordahl Lelandais was later charged with her abduction and murder. This opened old wounds about the discussion on the right for an adult to just disappear. It would seem that Lelandais was further linked to other unsolved disappearance and murders. Was he a serial killer? In France there are around 1,000 unidentified bodies found each year. Furthermore, France does not maintain a national database of DNA or documents for such bodies. Nor DNA in a national database for missing people and relatives (As at 2018)

Moreover, the right for an adult to disappear would leave a gate wide open for serial killers, killers, traffickers and abductors. It's like opening your supermarket doors and letting such people take what they want without any follow up.

I believe that the right to remain missing should be removed. Or at least until the adult is found and questioned by police and a medical professional. If found in sane mind, then their right to go about their business is their choice. However there are too many people who are suffering from mental health issues and as such they become missing not on their own accord but that of the mental health issue that they are facing.

"United Nations and European Union crime data show that more people are murdered in France than its neighbours – France:

*(population 82.7 million) has an average of 801 people that were murdered. Plus there are around 1,000 unidentified bodies discovered in France every year. These bodies are buried without the state gathering any DNA or documentation, 2018"*

After the abduction and subsequent murder of Maëlys de Araujo (known as the girl in the white dress). Lelandais was then thought of as a possible serial killer after confessing to the murder of a solider that he had picked up while "thumbing" a lift back to his army barracks. The right to remain missing, gives such murderers the freedom to operate with little help coming for those who are truly missing.

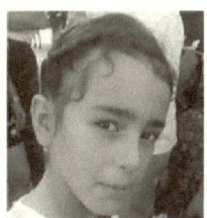

The murder of Mayes, is sickening and sad, but her death was not in vain it highlighted the need for France to rethink its laws on the right to remain missing. It is extremely sad, and of no comfort to the parents, that a child's death has to be the source of change, but this is the sad case in many instances.

I believe that we need a worldwide national database greater than Interpol and with powers that can extend past borders to track down people who are a threat to children or adults, by that I mean a person or organisation that has the capability to abuse, harm, commit murder, abduct or traffics a child or adult into the sexual, industrial or illegal adoption trade.

# Exploited

**CEOP:** Exploited is an 18-minute film which helps young people learn to stay safe from sexual exploitation. It educates young people to identify features of an exploitative friendship or relationship in contrast with the development of a healthy relationship, and gives them clear information about how to report abuse and access support.

https://www.youtube.com/watch?v=qORv-TgI4JI

## NRCDV.ORG Toolkit

The QR code below takes you to a website dedicated for runaway and homeless youths. While it is a toolkit designed for advocates in that domain, it does present information and resources that could benefit people who have been affected by runaways, homelessness or domestic and sexual assault.

## Support line

The website of the QR image below, contains areas of support for runaways, missing, and those contemplating becoming a runaway. It also contains many other useful resources and agencies that can help and provide you with information.

## What to do when a person goes missing.

Remember there is no mandatory waiting period. You do not have to wait 24 hours. Or indeed if you suspect that there has been an abduction. PHONE IMMEDIATELY do not wait even for a second.

1. Immediately Phone the Police
2. Phone 116000 and report your child missing {free 24 hour hotline, missing persons alert]
3. Seal of the area if you suspect an abduction
4. Get photographs of the missing person make copies and pass them out. Get help to do this
5. If you have a photo of the missing person on your phone then send (WhatsApp, or any other platform) to everyone that is helping you.
6. Get a friend to make a list of everyone that is helping you. Name, address, Telephone number, even a photograph of them.
7. Get help to search the surrounding areas
8. Take photos of everything and anything around you and as you go on your search.
9. Get the newspapers, TV and radio to broadcast details urgently.
10. Keep HOPE in your heart

## Report a missing person in immediate danger

## Call 999 Immediately and 116000

The following is from the met.police.uk/ website. Please have the following information ready, if possible.

- Date and time the person was last seen and who by.
- What they were wearing when they were last seen.
- Their description, such as height, colouring, marks or scars.
- Their address.
- Any family, friends, or places they often go.
- Do they have access to a car? If yes, please have the registration number, if possible.
- Other means of transport (do they have a bus or rail card?)
- Any enquiries that have been made to find out the person's whereabouts.
- Any vulnerabilities they have, such as medical needs or a disability?
- Why you consider them to be in immediate danger.

Even if you're not sure, we'd rather hear from you and make the decision ourselves.

## Details to help you search for someone
1) Keep yourself safe and well.
2) Get help from friends, family and anyone willing to help you
3) Take photos of everything that you see while searching, regardless. Don't even think about what you are photographing. (Applies immediately after the child/person has gone missing)
4) Call Hospitals and homeless centres
5) Contact Their Friends and Family
6) Use social media to ask for help
7) Check Their Social Media Accounts
8) Keep in regular contact with the Police
9) Ask the Community for help
10) Make Posters
11) Contact Missing People Resources [missingpeople.org.uk] and any others you know of locally and further afield]
12) Take notes and/or photos of the street names that have been searched.
13) Search in barren areas, areas where work is being carried out.
14) Make a list of places you think that they might turn to or go to
15) Go to missingpeople.org.uk and sign up for a missing child alert. They only send out alerts to the missing in your area,

# A story of Hope

Kenneth Howard a twenty two month old baby boy was rescued from a fifty feet slope after searchers heard him crying. The search lasted three days and involved helicopters, drones and thermal cameras.

It is believed that he wandered off three days earlier and had become trapped on the cliff side. *[May 2019 in the USA]*

This is what I call a God Dilemma. It is also proof that we ask too much from a god created by humans as a means of trying to make an understanding out of your existence and usually done at any cost to humanity.

*Kenneth's mother, Tasha said: "It's been difficult. But I never did give up, because I had faith. I had faith, and I know God is with us because we wouldn't have found him."*

Of course the mother is overjoyed and thankful, but ask yourself one question.

What about the many thousands of other missing children and adults?

Where they not found because God was not with them?

# Adverse Childhood Experiences (ACE's)

An understanding of ACE's can further highlight the dangers to you and your children. It will address how you react to your own child in times of stress and how your own personal Adverse Childhood Experiences that you suffered as a child can shape your social interactions, your relationships and indeed interactions with your own children.

It's not too late, resilience can be built to alter your current journey towards your impending future.

It is necessary to discuss the impact that adverse childhood experiences can have on your children and how these adversities can then manifest into adulthood and beyond.

Parents who incurred adversity when they were a child can pass that trauma on to their own children and so forth. Thus becoming an intergeneration problem.

These issues are equally compounded by the immense pressure put on children by family, peer pressures, school pressures and a lack of understanding towards the youth in our society.

Adversity in childhood holds the source of the majority if not all of the problems we all face in later life. Up to recently we have been trying to fix or medicate the symptoms. The ACE study now leads us to understand the source of the problems. This helps us to be able to better fix oneself through attacking the source of our mental health issues and by developing resilience towards these adversities without the need for medication. Sometimes medication maybe the only option, but in reality medications major setback is that they can really fuck with your brain and body The labels are loaded with side effects, and you and your medical advisors have to choose what would be the best decision.

Today people can talk more freely about 'things' that happen in their home without the need for the 'hush-hush' attitude of keeping what happens to you firmly within the home.

Moreover, it is never too late, while Adverse Childhood Experiences shape your experiences into adult hood, you can reshape your mental health as an adult and reduce the sources of your problems. You will never change what has happened, but you can address the source and make amends through a process of developing resilience.

Furthermore, your own understanding of ACE's can help you mend your ways towards your children and give them the healthy upbringing that they need and deserve.

Go to https://www/missinginparis.com and complete the ACE survey. The higher the score the higher your exposure has been to adversity as you grew up. Without any form of resilience this could cause health problems. But remember, you are not defined by your ACE score, but rather your score will allow you to define where your behaviour originated and by acknowledging this you can then begin to build resilience and change your life for the better.

These questions could re-open old wounds and draw past memories and as such contact help numbers are provided in the event that the questions make you become overwhelmed. Phone the help lines and talk to someone who can listen and help you. You could always complete the questionnaire with a supportive friend.

The questions you will be asked on the online survey are totally anonymous and are listed below. This ACE survey has been changed to adapt to the true community aspect of Adverse Childhood Experiences that being, the home, education, religion and society.

Mental health issues can be created by your childhood experiences this subsequently manifests into adulthood and develops the traits of dysfunction and disease.

This pattern of self-destruction is further introduced to your own children and the cycle continues over and over again. Until it is broken by children or adults who develop resilience against these destructing forces. Likewise, adults can still learn resilience techniques to help them live a better life and assist their own children in becoming at one with themselves in a world that's turbulent, chaotic and fast paced.

There is no place in society for adversity, the time for change is now.

# ACE's

## Introduction

I have been researching Adverse Childhood Experiences (ACE's) over the last four years and have included parts of my diploma thesis within this book.

The ACE Study is an ongoing collaboration originally between the Kaiser Permanente's Department of Preventive Medicine in San Diego and the CDC (Disease Control and Prevention) unit. Moreover, today this collaboration has grown to other countries since its original concept in 1985.

Dr Felitti is a specialist in preventive medicine and he initially discovered this medical breakthrough while helping obese people lose weight through a positive choice program. He discovered that the people who were dropping out of his program and going back to their old habits were people who displayed success in losing weight. As a result he decided to investigate further and began a study with 286 obese people. In this study he discovered that their obesity was being used as a barrier to unwanted sexual attention or physical abuse. He further discovered by asking a question in error that many of the people being questioned had been physically or sexually abused as a child.

This further highlighted the severity of the problem since these types of questions were normally taboo in the medical world. The results of the questions further demonstrated that the child's developing brain can be damaged as a result of this adversity (Toxic Stress).

He further found that in many instances food was not the obese persons first choice, some tried tobacco, alcohol, and drugs to help them forget and reduce the stress and pain. Dr Robert Anda, of the CDC, around the same time was also studying health problems that included patients with the following abuses, smoking, alcohol, obesity, drugs, and high risk sexual behaviours.

As a result Dr Anda and Dr Felitti combined their research and developed a large scale epidemiologic study involving over 17,000 people. This study asked questions in relation to their traumatic and adverse childhood experiences. The questions asked in this study had never been imposed by the medical profession on any other person before. These questions were prying into the household of the person and their relationship with their carer(s). The ACE study formed three distinct areas of Emotional, Physical and sexual abuse questions. And further broke down into areas of (a) Abuse (b) Neglect and (c) Household Dysfunction.

This survey outcome outlined that traumatic and stressful childhood experiences not only shaped behaviours, but overwhelmingly underlined them as leading causes of social problems, health related problems, and causes of early death. The ACE Study was designed to access multiple types of abuse, neglect, domestic violence, and serious household dysfunction at the same time.

Mechanism by Which Adverse Childhood Experiences Influence Health and Well-being Throughout the Lifespan

The Study demonstrated that an unexpectedly high number of these people had experienced significant abuse or household dysfunction during their childhood.

During the study it was found that several of the questions in the ACEs questionnaire related to occurrences that a child experienced in their child's home. This led to what is called the ACEs scoring system. Each participant was attributed one point for each question of adverse childhood experience occurring prior to age 18 on each of the 10 questions.

The ACE score was used as a measure for the exposure to a traumatic childhood. It was further linked to an increase in the use of drugs, tobacco and alcohol abuse if you had an ACE score of 3 or more.

The stress and traumatic events as outlined in the ACEs study demonstrated the impact of childhood trauma in later life as an adult. These events trigger an adversity in learning, cognition and social relationships within the child suffering from this trauma. Furthermore, this manifests itself in later life and certain occurrences, such as smells or sounds can trigger an event to be relived, and this increases ongoing stress. Too much or continuous traumatic stress can have a detrimental outcome in the cognition of a developing child.

However, while we cannot change the past it has been discovered that the brain is pliable to change and repair and as such it has been termed "plastic." Moreover, this allows us to teach methods of resilience via several types of programs, such as Mindfulness, CBT, and Holistic approaches.

It has been further studied and discovered that rather than develop resilience only for the child that is experiencing adversity at home, it should be rolled out as a whole community approach. This approach is being adopted in Scotland, Wales and the North of Ireland. Understanding the adversities that a child is experiencing allows the teacher, educator or others in the community to be aware of any detrimental impacts of their actions towards a child. Moreover, it could assist the carer/parent in understanding their motives and aid them in stopping this abuse. Furthermore, it has been proven that even a significant and positive person such as a teacher, other family member, and friend in a child's life can sway the child towards a sustainable level of resilience.

The original study did not take into account education and religion as a factor of adversity in childhood. As you will read later education and religion can also create adversity in children. Therefore I have developed an adaptation of the original ACE survey, to include school and religion.

Since children spend a vast amount of time in the education system, it is extremely important that a model towards a whole school approach is developed and rolled out in all schools. More importantly this approach should encompass every person in the school and not just the children experiencing adversity in the home. Moreover, it should also include the parents/carer, peers and community. By doing so, we have a better chance of reducing trauma in the child, triggers in the adult and a vast reduction in the cost of future treatment and the budgets of our governments.

In conclusion, it is fundamental to try and understand stress and its development on childhood development. While some stress is good for the body the ACE study has found that many people who are undergoing trauma and disease in their lives have been exposed to an unhealthy dose of stress in their childhood. Stress can be further analysed into positive stress (Brief increases to heart rate and mild elevation of stress hormones), Tolerable stress (Such as a death in the family, serious illness or injury, but this stress can be aided by a positive influence or relationship in the child's life) Toxic Stress (Intense and prolonged levels of stress without any positive relationship in the child's life).

The ACE study has had a tremendous impact on other countries and as such the questionnaire has been adapted to meet the needs of children who have experienced wars and country specific internal conflict. Furthermore, it has been proven that children who have lived or are living through conflict can pass on this trauma to their children via their DNA. This knowledge of historical passing on of trauma and stress throughout generations will allow a further working model of Hope and resilience to be developed that encompasses a whole community approach to solving this worldwide problem. Moreover, having a 'significant other' in a child's life is hope and resilience.

Resilience forms an important part of protecting a child from ACE's.

It is considered that if a child has at least one positive and caring adult in their life then that can build a foundation of consistency and offers a layer of resilience for the child. That person can be a teacher, a coach at the football club, a relative, one parent and so forth.

As a teacher you need to spot the signs and ensure that the child views you as a person of trust that they can turn to for resilience. Be there for them and listen to what they have to say.

## Adverse Childhood Experiences (ACES's)

**The Northern Ireland ACE Animation** forms the basis of raising awareness of adverse childhood experiences in Northern Ireland and how you can be the change to support children, their families or adults impacted by childhood adversity.

**Public Health Network Cymru -** Adverse Childhood Experiences (ACEs) are traumatic events that affect children while growing up, such as suffering child maltreatment or living in a household affected by domestic violence, substance misuse or mental illness.

# Teen Brain Development

*NIDA explores in this video the intriguing similarities between the processes of brain development and computer programming. The analogy helps us understand why toxic environmental factors like drugs, bullying, or lack of sleep can have such a long-lasting impact on a teenager's life and can be used to empower your children or students with information they need make better decisions. Extract from NDA]*

A Teenager's Brain is still developing, something that most adults forget. Our institutions (schools, police, and courts) sometimes take a dogmatic view of a teenager, when in fact studies have proven that a teenager's brain is still developing right up to mid or late twenties. This can have severe consequences on how the teenager will deal with problems that can occur in their life such as, relationships, peer, school, religious pressures and risk taking.

Teenagers break the rules because their immature brains aren't wired to properly respond to reward or punishment.

Researchers have discovered that the Adolescent brain is less likely to respond to punishments and incentives due to the fact that their brains are still configuring themselves and are not yet fully developed.

Most parents and teachers can easily see that? It's almost impossible to get teenagers to focus on what you want them to do regardless of how you try and make them do what is asked.

Therefore, you need to change your methods of getting a child to respond, make it fun and interesting and mitigate a level of risk taking in the approach to the teenagers learning (such as public speaking in the class etc.)

Scan the QR code below to watch Dr Siegel's hand model describing the brain.

Dr Siegel describes in the video above how a teenager can 'flip their lid' due to that part of the brain not being fully developed yet.

Moreover, an adult can do the same in times of anger or stress. But if you understand why you are doing this then you could be able to bring yourself back to your normal state and avoid this unnecessary stress or confrontation.

# ACE Survey
## Missing in Paris Adaptation

### Circle the appropriate answer below:
And please go to https://www.missinginparis.com and complete the survey below, it is totally anonymous.

## While you were growing up, during your First 18 years of life:

### General Questions:

**QA.** Did you **ever** attend a single denomination school (meaning a school that had one religious belief)?

Yes    No

**QB.** What is your sex?

Girl    Boy

**QC.** Did you every live in a foster or care home?

Yes    No

**QD.** Have you ever had an abortion?

Yes    No    Yes, I was forced to have an abortion

**QD.** Have you ever spent 1 hour or more per day over 3 months or more on Social Media Platforms?

Yes    No

**QE.** Have you ever thought about committing suicide?

Yes     No

**QF.** Did you ever attempt suicide?

Yes     No

## Household ACE's

**Q1.** Did a parent or other adult in the household **often** ... Swear at you, insult you, put you down, or humiliate you? **Or Act in a way** that made you afraid that you might be physically hurt?

Yes     No

**Q2.** Did a parent or other adult in the household **often**... Push, grab, slap, or throw something at you? **Or ever hit you** so hard that you had marks or were injured?

Yes     No

**Q3.** (Applies if you were under the age of sexual consent) Did an adult **ever**... Touch or fondle you or have you touch their body in a sexual way? Or Try to or actually have oral, anal, or vaginal sex with you?

Yes     No

**Q4.** Did you **often** feel that ... No one in your family loved you or thought you were important or special? Or your family didn't look out for each other, feel close to each other, or support each other?

Yes    No

**Q5.** Did you **often** feel that ... You didn't have enough to eat, had to wear dirty clothes, and had no one to protect you? Or your parents were too drunk or high to take care of you or take you to the doctor if you needed it?

Yes    No

**Q6.** Were your parents **ever:** separated or divorced or relationship totally broke up? [This applies to children whose parents were either married or non-married but where in a full time relationship before the breakup]

Yes    No

**Q7.** Was your mother, stepmother, father or stepfather: **Often** pushed, grabbed, slapped, or had something thrown at her/him? Or **sometimes or often** kicked, bitten, hit with a fist, or hit with something hard? **Or Ever** repeatedly hit over at least a few minutes or threatened with a gun or knife?

Yes    No

**Q8.** Did you live with anyone in your family who was a problem drinker or alcoholic or who used street drugs?

Yes    No

**Q9.** Was any household member depressed or mentally ill or did any household member attempt suicide?

Yes    No

**Q10.** Did a household member go to prison?

Yes    No

## Education – Religion ACE's

**Q11.** Did any teacher or other adult in your school **often** ... Swear at you, insult you, put you down, or humiliate you? Or Act in a way that made you afraid that you might be physically hurt?

Yes    No

**Q12.** Did a teacher or other adult in your school **often** ... Push, grab, slap, or throw something at you? Or ever hit you so hard that you had marks or were injured?

Yes    No

**Q13.** Did a teacher or other adult at your school **ever** ... Touch or fondle you or have you touch their body in a sexual way? Or Try to or actually have oral, anal, or vaginal sex with you?

Yes    No

**Q14.** Did you **often** feel that ... teachers in your school made you think that you were unimportant or useless or stupid?

Yes    No

**Q15.** Where you ever taught by a teacher who was drunk or on drugs?

Yes    No

**Q16.** Did your teacher: **Often** push, grab, slap, or throw something at you? Or **sometimes or often** hit you, or hit you with something hard?

Yes    No

**Q17.** Did your school ever send you home or keep you from attending school as a form of disciplinary action, for example suspension?

Yes    No

**Q18.** Where you **often** punished by having to write religious words or sentences in a book at school?

Yes    No

**Q19** Were there **ever** regular arguments on doing homework between you and your parents/carers which resulted in you having really bad feelings about yourself?

Yes    No

**Q20** Were you **ever** given disciplinary action for not completing your homework by being made to stay later in school, or by suspension or by writing lines of words on paper?

Yes    No

**Q21.** Did a religious leader or other adult at your church **ever**... Touch or fondle you or have you touch their body in a sexual way? Or Try to or actually had oral, anal, or vaginal sex with you?

Yes    No

**Q22** Were you **often** forced to attend church or were shouted at to attend a religious service?

Yes   No

**Society**

Q23 Where you ever caught up in a war, coup, hostility, internal conflict, or anything that involved ongoing violence, or any other event that included a possibility of harm?

Yes   No


The General questions and School/Religious/Society questions were never part of the original ACE questionnaire or survey. However, children spend a large portion of their time at school and possibly church. Therefore, I feel it is important that we gauge what is happening within these closed door institutions.

While the majority of teachers and religious leaders are "thoughtful, caring and educationally supportive" to our children, we cannot turn a blind eye to what is going on within these organisations. Nor can they be exempt from their responsibility in creating Adverse Childhood Experiences within our children. As such I developed the questions above to bring to light adversities that our children have experienced within their school and religion. Moreover, the only way to stop Adverse Childhood Experiences, is through a community wide approach involving every organisation that comes into contact with children and young adults, such as schools, religion, police, courts, prisons and the community as a whole.

Question 22 above arose from evidence that many children were abused by continual shouting followed by slapping, by parents or religious leaders in order to make their children attend a religious services. Furthermore, parents could be out-casted by others in the community for not forcing religion onto their children. Parents would also be given words of doom and gloom from leaders informing them that they would be going to hell if they did not attend their religious service. Such actions are a major factor to the mental health of all children and adults who have suffered such fate at the hands of thoughtless and inconsiderate religious books of reference and that of its leaders.

# The Education System

At the age of twelve years old and up until I left school, teachers were allowed to carry out physical punishments.

Punishment methods included, crossing both hands and stretching them out in front of the teacher. The teacher would place a two to three feet in length and ¼ inch thick leather belt behind their shoulder. And with an almighty swing from their shoulder the belt would smack into the crossed hands of the pupil. The pain was excruciating and in many cases blood tricked from our hands or wrists. The teacher would often provide two swings per child, making the child change their hand over, thus ensuring that both hands were hit by the belt (This was the method I was punished with at my school.) In some other schools as in the Isle of Man a birch was used as a form of physical punishment. Some other schools in the UK and Ireland would get the child to bend down and the teacher would smash a cane against their bum.

Thankfully these types of punishment are now classified as physical abuse. However, in some countries physical abuse against a child is still acceptable as a form of punishment and control.

Shouting and belittling a child still goes on in our schools by uncaring and thoughtless teachers, this is abuse. Abuse that can no longer be tolerated. Talk with your child and listen to what they have to say, don't brush it off with, "well you deserved that". Do something about this form of abuse, speak with your school principal and the safeguarding officer, make your concerns clear and if they don't listen take legal action against the school, the board of governors and the local school authority. We can't let our education establishment get away with abuse any more, STOP ABUSE NOW.

My children were abused by teachers at school on several occasions, both in primary and secondary school.

In secondary school, my son created a drawing that the teacher thought was inappropriate. At first she crumpled it up and threw it in the bin. As my son was leaving the classroom, she called him back and took the crumpled drawing from the bin, opened it up and said I'm phoning your mum. The teacher then put my child in a room and shut the door. Making sure that he could see her talk to his mum but not hear the conversation. Then she would open the door so that he could hear part of the conversation and again she would close the door. This was repeated several times. However, the teacher never mentioned the drawing to his mum, nor did she mention that our son was present while they spoke. The teacher in front of our son also asked his mum if there was anything wrong with him. When our son came home from school he had anxiety and stress and wondered what he had done that was so very bad.

Later that afternoon I received a phone call from a male teacher, who explained about the drawing. Well actually he could not explain, I asked him several times to outline the drawing but he couldn't. He was embarrassed to use real words like 'Vagina' and 'Penis' to describe a part of a human body. And this is a secondary school teacher? Are schools not aware of the development of a teenager? Do teachers not understand the brain development of a teenager and the risk behaviours that are associated with their raging and developing hormones?

The female teacher, being a person in authority, committed abuse. When it was challenged at school the teacher miraculously became ill and was absent for the parent-school meeting only to return a few weeks later, hoping that the problem blew away with the thunderstorm.

The teacher managed to escape any punishment that she clearly deserved. Yet my son's mental health suffered. Moreover, the teacher has a union and an educational support system in place to keep the parents at bay. Yet the child has very little instant support, no one is really fighting the battles for our children in schools.

The police said that this is a matter for the school and education board. Now let's stop right there for a second!! Does that not sound very familiar? When I was a child the police would be called out to families were the father was hitting the mother or vice versa. The police response was that it is 'domestic' and they cannot get involved. Thankfully times have changed and they do attend to domestic violence and actually do something about it. How many years have to pass before the police will get involved in abuse at school? It has been documented many times in academic papers that verbal and emotional abuse has severe consequences to the brain development of a child.

In primary school my daughter was pulled out of her class by the scruff of her hair and was constantly belittle by the teacher. The principal of the school promised that this would never happen again and despite many visits to the school and letters to the board of governors to fix this and other problems nothing concrete ever happened. We were given the run-around, with many different types of excuses including a pile of bureaucratic procedures and so called 'red tape.'

*[If I had walked into my Childs school and pulled the teacher out of her classroom by the scruff of her hair, I would be in front of a magistrate at our local court. How can teachers think for one second that they have any authority or right to emotionally or physically harm a child? Simple answer, because they get away with it and in some cases your child is not able to verbalise this abuse. And these types of teachers are able to pass their abuse towards your child off as "your child has behaviour problems." Teachers who do such atrocities should not be teaching.]*

Months turned into years and as time passed quickly we had somehow allowed that teacher to avoid any major repercussions whatsoever.

Our children do not attend that school anymore however, we heard recently that she is up to her old tricks of abuse towards other children.

Gladly the majority of teachers are not like that, most I believe are caring, supportable, encouraging and help a child spread their wings. My son has an another teacher at his school who takes the time to understand his needs and that of the learning styles of everyone in his classroom, he also makes learning interesting and fun.

Teachers are limited to how they can help a child, they are forced to educate and teach in a manner that demands results at any cost and in classrooms that are overfilled with pupils.

Forty years has passed since I was in secondary education but nothing much has changed since my days. Yet technology, businesses and our society have changed dramatically. Our education institution is more concerned with grades and statistics of achievements, so much so that they encourage more kids to drop out of their school than to stay. These underachievers are in fact smarter in many other ways.

Jeremy Clarkson did not get any 'A' levels. Bill gates the co-founder of Microsoft dropped out of college after two years. Furthermore, those children that do make it to college or university are further penalised by having to pay for their education, creating a financial mental health problem even before they start work. And one that will follow them from college for the next 10 to 20 years until they make their final repayment.

These are barriers that affect the mental health of your child. Your school via the current educational system is directly affecting your child's self-esteem and mental wellbeing. They force your child to achieve regardless of the cost to their mental health. They increase the complexity of exams each year, so much so that 200 children committed suicide in the UK in 2017 directly as a result of their exams. And thousands more children developed high levels of anxiety and stress.

The educational system is not developing the child, they are stifling the child through a pure lack of understanding of the individual needs of the child. And they use the parents as a tool to achieve their aims, no wonder children turn to alcohol and drugs.

You send your children to school to be educated and not to be abused. The education system needs to be radically changed. A pathway to change would be to review the School system in Finland. That could be a fresh start to a new education system for schools and our children's wellbeing. Take the Finland model and make it even better for your countries children.

**Finland Education**, extracts from Centre of Public Impact: *"Education is included as a basic right in the constitution of the country, evidence of its importance to all the political actors in Finland. "Public authorities must secure equal opportunities for every resident in Finland for study and self-development, according to their abilities, irrespective of their place of residence, language or financial status....Finland engaged in a process of gradual reform to make the country's education system serve the whole country. The quality of its teachers and the achievements of its students now make it the envy of the world...The quality of teachers and teaching lies at the heart of Finland's educational success."*

My son came to his mum and showed her two videos, he said *"why can't our schools be creative and encourage children to grow?"* Teachers have the best job in the planet, they have the ability to take a child and let their dreams and aspirations come true. Yet if the child does not fit into the educational system of predefined slots and tests then the child is classified as stupid or non-compliant.

I do not believe in transfer tests, I believe that they should be scrapped. I don't believe that the tax payer should pay for one child to go to a "better" school because of their marks and the other child to go to a school classified as "worse" This is a reflection of the past were one child got a better education at the cost of the many that did not.

Against our mindful reasoning, our daughter did her transfer test, her mark was 84%, however in order to curtail the number of children getting into the schools that require a transfer test, the results students got were aggregated and averaged so she got a lower mark. Even in university, you don't get treated like that.

**Possible Solutions:** First and foremost look at the education system in Finland and build our education around their model but make it even better.

Rather than have tables and seats in rows in the classroom, why don't we **have seats in a circle** so that everyone in the class can see each other and be fostered to collaborate with the response that no answer is wrong or stupid and pave the way for a more 'holistic' approach to education.

**Homework is one of the curses** within our current educational institution. Children don't like it and nor do parents. The number of children that are abused, shouted at, made to feel stupid by parents and teachers over homework is alarmingly too high. My initial solution to homework: Reduce each subject on the timetable by 10 mins. At the end of the normal school day, that last class is homework class. In that class the children have a teacher who can actually help the child succeed, by offering constructive and helpful teaching to assist with homework. Many parents are unable to help or don't have the knowledge or capacity to help their child with their homework. This results in the child getting punished at school by teachers and punished again at home by parents. That indeed is not a creative, encouraging or healthy situation for a child to be in.

Saku Tuominen, director of the HundrEd project in in Finland says parents in Finland don't really want longer hours in school. He further states that there is a "holistic" approach to education, with parents wanting a family-friendly approach. Do your own research on the subject, but suffice to say that Finland has been reshaping its education system since the 1970 and giving teachers more autonomy, thus parents are trusting the teachers and schools more. As far as ACE's are concerned I fully believe that homework is one of the major cause of friction and ACE's in families between child and parent and between parent and parent and between child and School, but not so in Finland.

**Suicide and Mental Health:** The amount of pressure put on our children by the education system is tantamount to neglect and abuse. No wonder many children drop out of school, turn to drugs, commit suicide and have mental health issues.

https://papyrus-uk.org/ have stated that 'Two hundred of our school children are lost every year to suicide.'

Do we need exams? Do we need GSCE's? (After all children don't leave at 16 anymore, nor do employers take these qualifications seriously.) Children now leave school at 18, therefore our antiquated education system is a breeding ground for the new era and future for mental health issues.

Exams should be replaced by course work and getting out to the workplace and to see practical examples.

Every year in May and then in August, our children await those dreaded brown envelopes that contain the virus of mental health issues. When opened a child can be catapulted into all sorts of feelings, thoughts and emotions.

Schools are great at showing-off their statistics of how well they have done, why not get each school to publish how many children have committed suicide or developed mental health issues as a result of their education at that school? Then as a parent you will know what school to truly avoid.

For the 200 children that take their own lives each year in the UK, their journey on earth is sadly over. The current system needs to take some of the blame. If you are a parent, help your child...do not belittle your child for not getting the results that YOU desired, support them, give them understanding and love and if they fail or do not get the marks they wanted, remind them it's not the end of the world.

Young minds, have this to say on disappointing exam results:

https://youngminds.org.uk/blog/dealing-with-disappointing-exam-results/

*"You have so many options. Your school might not tell you all of them, or they might make some options seem better than others. But everyone has a different idea of what success looks like, so*

different options will be best for different people. You are no less than your peers for choosing a different route to them. You are not inferior, or less intelligent, or less ambitious. You are creating your own route to your own version of success and that is the smartest decision you can make. By Irum, Activist"

"So if your results are not what you hoped for, stay calm, research your options, and don't beat yourself up. Try to comfort yourself in the same way you would comfort your best friend. Be kind to yourself. Give yourself a break. You are good enough. Those letters/numbers are not the most important thing in the world. If it's not far too cheesy and cliché, remind yourself that everything happens for a reason, and that everything will turn out okay. Don't give up on your dreams or yourself.

I like this quote by author Napoleon Hill: 'Most great people have attained their greatest success just one step beyond their greatest failure.'"

As a parent please read above and apply it to your thinking, your child is never a failure regardless, full stop!

I have digressed yet again, but I needed to point the above out as exam and result times are so stressful. Plus today I saw many children with their brown envelopes in their hands and many with sad faces.

Research has proved that schools and religion play an important role due to the contact it has with our children and as such can contribute to the adversity of a child. Therefore the Missing in Paris adaptation ACE survey will include questions that cover both educational and religion.

The ACE survey can lead a person to discover why they do what they do. Every event in a developing child's life affects them right into adulthood.

North of Ireland Schools are supposed to become ACE and trauma aware by 2020. And in my mind the only way that they will fully accomplish this is by drastically changing the way that they are directed to teach our children by an educational establishment that should be torn down from the core and rebuilt with children in mind. Moreover, schools must stop being allowed to make statistics more important than that of the children they are supposed to be educating.

A child's mental health is far more important than that of an education system driven by results at any cost. Children and parents are sold the dream that the higher an education the better the job that they will get. The dream that our education and government try to sell you, is actually a shooting star of a dream. It's false and unrealistic. That's why today you will find many university graduates working in jobs that certainly do not require the level of education that they have, this is another cause of mental health issues. You spend four years working on a university degree, with debt up to your eyes and you're in a job were you don't even earn enough money to pay back your student loan.

Judge Lady Rafferty, (14th August 2018) turned down the application to hold the current Prime Minister of the UK responsible and accountable for the lies and deceit that Boris Johnson branded about while campaigning for the leave BREXIT campaign. She further stated that the person on the street can make their own minds up on the truth of what Politian's say.

Not only is this a crooked outrage, but our legal system with no common sense and morale decency has implied that anyone in a position of power can lie and deceive the public in any manner or form that they want. What does that teach your child?

Not only that, our children as students are sold the idea that they too can become a Top Paid Judge , and this justifies the unjustifiable push on our children towards exams. However in reality there were 2.34 million students in higher education (according to Universities UK, 2017/2018) but you can only have One Top Judge, you can only have One Prime Minister, you can only have one 'so called top of anything.' Therefore your child has 1 in 2.34 million chance of becoming a top of anything (that's crude statistics without taking into account all the other years and student numbers in and out of education.) Yet that is a driving factor for education at any cost. If you do the lottery you have a 1 in 7,509,579 chance of getting five numbers plus the bonus ball.

**All Education should be totally free without any charge whatsoever. The UK education system needs re-built from the foundation upwards.**

I'm not a number, I'm a free person (Guess what TV program that's from?)

# What is School for? By Prince EA

There is no doubt that our educational system needs to be overhauled. Currently the system is 'sucking in' all children to find the few children that will succeed, (as defined by such institutions defined rules) before spewing the rest out as rejects. University graduates are in debt for the next fifteen to twenty years, what a great way to curb education for everyone, what a great way for a teenager to start their career, stressed to the hilt. And that is the UK education system for you. As such I firmly believe that the education institutions are one of the major contributors to Adverse Childhood Experiences

# School Principal Reacts to Prince EA

## I JUST SUED THE SCHOOL SYSTEM

My Son showed the Prince EA video to his mum and asked "Why can't our school be like this. I might not be able to get the grades that my teachers are pushing me relentlessly to achieve. But I'm smart just in a different way?" At 12 years of age my son was smart enough to realise that the current education system is not truly educational. That brought tears to our eyes.

Children are being abused to achieve results at any cost to their mental health by an outdated and useless educational system. Furthermore when the child gets home from school, some parents pour out further abuse on their child for not studying enough and labelling their child as stupid. Both these statements are ACE's at a level of abuse.

# Tragic News re School and Religion

'Humiliated' teenager took his own life after being molested by sex-crazed female teacher who is now serving 20 years for having sex with four minors.

A 28-year-old female arts teacher from a Perth school is facing up to 20 years behind bars after pleading guilty to 48 sex offences against two of her female students.

Manchester's prized Chetham School of Music former school's director of music, Michael Brewer (also the founder of the National Youth Choir), and his wife were convicted for abusing a former pupil at the school in the 1970 and 1980s. The Victim Frances Andrade, was 14 when the abuse started at the independent boarding school. She died after giving evidence at the trial – it is believed she committed suicide. Police are now investigating claims of abuse at the school from more than 30 women.

BILLY Connolly has blamed the Catholic Church's opposition to divorce for his childhood abuse, claiming that the collapse of his parents' marriage turned his father into a "sexually frustrated" paedophile. The comedian, who was sexually abused from the age of 10, said that his father did not seek a divorce after his mother walked out because he was wracked by Catholic guilt. Connolly said his father, who believed in the sanctity of marriage, turned his sexual attentions to his son instead.

The Christian Brothers-educated judge believes cruel residential institutions existed in Ireland for so long as they did because the State was in thrall to the Catholic Church. The 2,600 page report, published a decade ago investigated 215 institutions which saw 170,000 under the age of 16 go through their hands between 1922 and the early 1970s. The commission, which was established in 2000, found that children had suffered neglect, physical and emotional abuse, while sexual abuse was endemic in all boys' institutions.

March 14, 2019, WARSAW — The Roman Catholic Church in Poland released long-awaited statistics on Thursday that shed light on the sexual abuse of children by 392 priests over the past 28 years.

The Guardian newspaper in May 2019 reported that Child sexual abuse in a wide range of religious organisations and settings, including Jehovah's Witnesses, Buddhists, is to be scrutinised in an official inquiry.

The investigation by the independent inquiry into child sexual abuse (IICSA) will review child protection and policies in organisations belonging to nonconformist Christian denominations, Baptists, Methodists, Islam, Judaism, Sikhism and Hinduism.

What is astounding is the demand for everyone to stop listening and purchasing Michael Jackson music when indeed he was only one person. Where is the demand against banning religions? After all thousands of its leaders have committed abuse long before and after Michael Jackson lived on this earth?

What makes one person want to ban Jackson's music and another person still attend religious services?

While the above might at first appear not to have anything to do with the missing, it does. ACE's affect the mentality of children and adults and in the majority of cases that's why they go missing. Furthermore, children in care who go missing are at a larger risk of being groomed or trafficked.

Many adults who commit these crimes have also been affected by adversities as a child. It's a dysfunctional wheel, and one that needs repaired, we can't allow this wheel of adversity to keep turning. The only way to repair this massive problem is to educate our children so that they understand NO means NO.

Regardless of who the abusers are, be it, a parent, family member, religious leader, school teacher, police officer or by any other person. A whole community approach to ACE's is the only way forward, everyone must come on board, and everyone must buy into this.

Billy Connelly touched on the mentality of offenders head on. Billie's father so consumed by the guilt of not wanting a divorce because his Catholic religion forbid it. His father then turned his sexual frustration on his son. Religious books are designed to control a person and certainly not to free them.

Of course that is not an excuse to sexually abuse your son, but it does demonstrate the power that religion can have on the mental health of a person who have possible mental health issues themselves.

In the case of suicide bombers, they believe via their God that they are doing great things. But in reality if your God demanded you to do terrible things to others, then that indeed must be a Devil masquerading as a God.

To the people who go to their church and pray every day, why not channel that energy into actually helping others. Would that not be a great Christian deed?

Despite all the praying done by many different religions, nothing changes, wars still rage, children are abused and trafficked, murders, rapes, violence, inequality, and a lack of freedom still occur throughout the world. Instead of prayer why don't people turn to each other with care, consideration and love? Bringing down barriers instead of building barriers. Joining the world as one in pure equality, true freedom and a world without boundaries or persecution. A world where every person on earth is totally equal in every way. A world were poverty and hunger do not exist. A world were Health comes before wealth.

# Divorce

It is recognised in the ACE study that when parents are divorced or separated then this can have a detrimental effect on children. I would further mention that the term married includes two people who live together and are bringing up a child. There is no difference whatsoever between married parents and parents who live together that raise a child. No difference whatsoever, apart from a piece of paper and legal chains around your ankles.

While it is ultimately better for a child to have both their natural parents present in their lives (married or unmarried) it is not always possible. If a child is brought up in a dysfunctional family, one that has parents constantly fighting and being abusive to themselves or their children, then indeed this is a travesty. And without any help or change to this dysfunctional pattern then the child and family would be better off if the parent's relationship ended and they parted ways. The child looks to adults for support, protection and nurturing, and when that is not available the family unit has broken down. The wellbeing of the child should always come first.

**The Country of Ireland** went to the polls in May 2019 to decide how long a person will remain married before they can seek a divorce. (Reducing the divorce from 4 years to 2 years) Ludicrous!

Is everyone blind? How dare any country, group or religion decide who can and cannot stay married. People are free, if you are in a dysfunctional relationship married or not, then you are entitled to leave immediately and as a free person. A married person is not at the hands of a public vote. Religion or government, in fact no one should ever be allowed to decide what a person should or can't do in a dysfunction relationship. The people in the relationship are the only ones that will decide. This is yet another form of abuse and control by a 'group' that can and will affect the mental health of the abused adult and that of their children.

**Best solution:** Don't get married and as such you are not giving such 'groups' any right to tell you what you can or cannot do.

**Interesting yet sick**, while Ireland voted to reduce the time for divorce from 4 years to 2 years they also voted to allow unborn child abortions up to 12 weeks.

# Abortion

Abortion, such a touchy and debatable subject and rightfully so. To end a human life that's hidden away in the depths of a woman's body is a long standing debate. And indeed is one of the pillars towards your future mental health. For taking an unborn life away could play on your mind. I personally blame society for pushing a mother to contemplate 'abortions of convenience.'

It is this fact of 'hidden from sight and not breathing earth's air' and only this fact that provides the legitimism for abortion.

The growing baby is not seen to the world apart from the growth of the women's womb. Hence, what is not seen is non-existent. When the baby breathes earth's air it becomes protected under the charter of the children's act. Until then it is only protected by the person growing the baby. Yet an attack on a pregnant women resulting in the death of the unborn baby is treated as a murder charge to the attacker. The abortion debate is confusing, don't you think?

In 2019 Ireland went to the public to vote for the right to end an unborn life. *[The right to an abortion exists in the UK and some other countries throughout the world. Women in Ireland who wanted an abortion either had to go to the UK to get it done or visit a person who was not qualified and that resulted in injury or death to the woman. Hence you can understand the vote.]* However, it was certainly weird when I watched the results in the news, with a MAN standing at the front of women announcing victory for women. For an instance in my imagination I saw the same man stand there holding a dead toddler in his victorious stretched out arm declaring, "I killed her as she no longer fits my lifestyle."

There are many reasons why a woman could seek an abortion, however while the scope of this book is towards the mental health of a person who decides to have an abortion I felt compelled to look at it further.

But regardless of anyone's beliefs ultimately the final outcome is at the hands of the person carrying the unborn baby or so law will try and dictate.

Religion has a knack of keeping its "flock" in line through emotional abuse and by providing the eyes of forgiveness via a confession. In reality a woman who has an abortion has gone against religion, however the confession clears them of that "religious sin," and all is forgiven. Confession is the creation of misery, for it intensifies injustices. Confessionals offer no morality whatsoever.

The only people that can forgive, are the person(s) who has been involved and yourself. Religion claims to have jurisdiction on confessions and forgiveness, but in reality this is yet another controlling feature of your life by a dysfunctional and manipulative group, hell bent in controlling you through fears of the unknown.

**The controversy to abortion**, is that the baby has not fully developed, and those in favour of abortion argue that it is not murder.

No one can prove when consciousness enters an embryo. Nor can anyone deny that it is not already there at the instant of the "big bang" of the "sperm and the egg's union." This uniting is indeed the creation of a new world, a world that takes the form of a human child. Hence woman are the gods of birth on earth.

If a child is conceived 'not wanted' then regardless of what a woman does, abortion or not, **the mental health of that woman could ultimately be altered in later years to come, and she/he (the mother and father of the aborted child) will need all the support and resilience that they can get.**

Having to decide on an abortion or not, must be one of the most soul destroying things for a woman to decide upon. My heart goes out to every person in this dilemma. But does it need to be a dilemma?

- Abortions were first forced on woman by religion and their persuasion on society to interpret having a child out of marriage as immoral, a deadly sin and having that child named as a Bastard if it's born.
- Women were raped and their freedom taken from them.
- Society treated single unmarried mothers as a disease.
- Women were at risk of death if their pregnancy came to term.
- Nowadays a child could be an inconvenience to a pleasure encounter that went wrong resulting in an unplanned or unwanted pregnancy.

**The main purpose of sex** is for reproduction. An abortion is an outcome of having sex. The intensity for sex and the pleasure it brings is so overwhelming that it overcomes all obstacles including those set by religion and society. After sex, these ridiculous rules laid down by religion and society consume a person's mind. So much so that even pre-martial and martial sex becomes a mental conundrum for those that believe in the concepts that such groups try to exert upon you.

For homosexuals and other minorities whose sexuality differs from that of a heterosexual group can feel ostracised by their religion and society. Indeed religion has no tolerance for these groups, in some countries it carries a death or lengthy jail sentence. For unmarried couples they are made to feel that they have sinned. And for the religious married couple they have sex for God, and the woman will submit to the man. Now how fucked up is that?

Religion takes the most natural of human acts and turns it around for their own purpose and aims. Such groups believe that if they can control your sexuality then they control the fabric of your existence.

What I find extremely puzzling, is that within the book called, "In the closet of the Vatican," the author claims that via interviews with priests, many of the priests including those in high places are homosexuals. And they choose religion as a way to hide that from the world. Yet their bible turns against homosexuals. The time for change is now, no longer can 'groups' be allowed to determine what you will or will not do in regards to a person's sexuality, nor can they make a woman second to a man.

Religions have enforced a no contraception rule, hence lots of unwanted pregnancies and abortions. Sex is personal to you, no one is allowed to tell you otherwise. Your choice is yours, have sex for pleasure or for conception or both, how you do it, where do it and why you do it, is your choice, and your choice alone, FULLSTOP.

This mentality on sex is another factor that can shape your mental health and push it towards an unhealthy balance. Never let anyone make you feel bad about having sex or your sexuality.

Christian society in the not so distant past forced unmarried mothers to have their babies torn away from the mother and given to a children's home or brought up with nuns or given to a more "deemed" worthy family. And all done in the name of religion.

- No wonder abortion is a contender on many women's minds, could you go through the mental health issues of having a child taken from you?
- No one has any right to judge an unmarried mother.
- No one has the right to name a child born out of wedlock a Bastard.

**The only true Bastards** are those that try to justify giving a child such a name. The real Bastards are our legal and religious groups that try to enforce such a name and meaning on to a child. These groups and any other person who attempts to label a child are the true Bastards of earth.

To those women who are thinking about abortion because of fashion or affecting their lifestyle or whom just can't be bothered, take a look in the mirror and see that your own life was the result of a birth and not an abortion. And don't let any person make you believe that you are not worthy, because you are!

**GET HELP: If you have had an abortion and this subject opens old wounds, talk with someone, get professional help, do not let it foster within your mind. Mistakes and bad judgements are made by everyone, but you can grow from it. You can't change what has happened in the past, but you can forge a good mental health for your future by seeking your own forgiveness within yourself.**

I discussed abortion more than I had intended to do, however the main point is that abortion can have a major effect on your mental health. Even those that do not have an abortion but really wanted an abortion, this to can have an impact on a person's mental health. It's a catch 22 situation. In reality, do not let the outside world dictate what you need to do (easier said than done).

On the flip side of abortion is 'birth then murder.' Atrocities towards Woman and child are not only in the history of religion. The Roman Empire had new born babies laid on the floor. The babies that were not picked up into the arms of the 'paterfamilias' where either murdered or sold for slavery. Women under such regimes were given legitimised independence after they gave birth to at least three live babies or four babies for slavery. Such statements make abortion look like kindergarten.

In times gone by you would have been out-casted for having a child out of wedlock. Even today the modern constraints that society force upon you, such as, all of the materialistic requirements to bring up a child (you need to work, you need to have money to afford your child and so forth) can lead you on a pathway of seeking an abortion. No wonder many woman want to turn to abortion. Abortion is a result of the pressures that (historical and present day) society, religion and governments have forced on each person's life, in particular women. Society needs to change drastically by putting people and families first and foremost, until then, abortion will be a requirement of many women at no fault to themselves. But done as a direct result of society pressures and expectations on the woman.

In 2018 (USA), Jennifer Clarey, murdered her 2 year old son, the judge made this statement. *"You were there to protect this child, and instead you were so reckless, so thoughtless, and so selfish so as to take this child's life before he had the chance to experience all life has to offer..."*

In 2018 (UK), Louise Porton, murdered her 17 month and 3 year old child. The judge stated that Louise had no medical history or mental health disorder. The distraught father claimed that her socialising, drinking, holiday and drugs made her children an Inconvenience to her.

Unlike the two devastating stories above, an aborted baby has never been given the chance to experience life on earth and sadly in many cases the baby is terminated not through illness or health risks to the mother but that of "being an Inconvenience to the mother and or father."

Abortion is an area of human life that can affect the mother and or father from day one, or it can come back many years later and haunt you. Seek help instantly if you have any feelings of regret.

Believe me, it's not your fault!

## How our Relationships Shape Us

This video is around 1 hour 40 minutes long, but well worth the time to watch and listen.

*Dr. Siegel's presentation. Dan Siegel, MD, is an internationally renowned neuropsychiatrist and New York Times bestselling author. He is the executive director of the Mindsight Institute, a professor at the UCLA School of Medicine, and the founding co-director of the Mindful Awareness Research Center at UCLA.*

# Drugs

Drugs are a major player on the pathway to childhood adversity. Drugs destroy families and communities. They assist criminals with funding other criminal activities, like pimp and forced prostitution, trafficking, weapons and increasing fear and power over others.

Drugs can appear to empower and give our young people a feeling of empowerment, happiness and joy in their lives. But in reality drugs destroy and maim our children. Your teenager may come home from a party and declare 'everyone is doing it.' So it's acceptable if everyone's doing it, right? You have others saying that it's like alcohol, it's now socially acceptable to do drugs, and if you don't you're an outcast. So how do you help your teenager through this difficult minefield?

Below are links to help you better understand the problems with drugs and drug addiction and how you can help your child through this?

Many children will tell you "I only tried it once, it's my life, I have to experience it, I'm a teenager, that's what teenagers do, but I won't do it again, I promise." Wrong, you need to keep an eye on the situation, if your child is hanging around with friends that are continually doing drugs then you need to be vigilant and make sure that your child is not being encouraged to do likewise. As mentioned earlier a teenagers brain is open for risk taking, this risk has to be managed, and not by shouting or blaming or name calling towards your child. If you do that then the child will not respond but could either go deeper into drugs or become a runaway. Be there as a listening non-judgemental ear for your child, and try and get them the help that they need to kick this soul destroying habit. Peer pressures can have a huge negative or positive impact on your child.

The legal system could do a lot more, instead of prosecuting the ones who are addicted and carrying small quantities of these drugs. They should catch the bigger fish and fry them.

I heard a story of a young lad just out of school who wanted to go to America. He had no money and no job prospects in his town. He had friends in America who offered him a job if he could get out there. So he went to the various authorities in his town to ask for financial assistance, but no one would help him.

He was then influenced to drop off drugs to other people to earn his fare out, he was caught. In court the judge decided to make an example of him and handed out a 21 month sentence. This young lads dreams are over, he will not be allowed into America, any possible employment will now not be forthcoming. He will most likely end up back in prison. The current prison setup cannot rehabilitate people effectively, but rather our prisons encourage a person to reoffend. This must be changed.

If the judge was ACE aware then perhaps he could have handled the matter in a different way, thereby giving the teenager a chance at life through programs of rehabilitation rather than incarceration. Moreover, the real criminals are the ones that are bringing the bulk of drugs into our countries. These criminals use underhand tactics to entice our youth to do their dirty work for them through intimidation, fear and claims for a better life and being free from poverty, so that they themselves don't get caught.

People do not realise the harm these substances can do to our youth. The teenager's brain is still developing. New studies have proved that the adolescent brain is still developing even into their late twenties.

Drugs to name only two, cannabis and cocaine. Disturbs the development of a teenager's brain which can lead to mental health issues.

Where do children buy these substances from? Are they getting them from older family members and friends or pushers who have befriended them? While peer pressures can be an influencing factor in leading a child towards drugs, there needs to be an active program of drug awareness and of self-esteem building for the child.

It's ok to say NO. And any person who does not listen to your NO's needs to be avoided.

*[The prefrontal cortex powers the ability to think, plan, solve problems, make decisions, and exert self-control over impulses. This is also the last part of the brain to mature, making teens most vulnerable. Shifting balance between this circuit and the reward and stress circuits of the basal ganglia and extended amygdala*

*make a person with a substance use disorder seek the drug compulsively with reduced impulse control. Extract taken from:* https://www.drugabuse.gov/publications/drugs-brains-behavior-science-addiction/drugs-brain]

The above QR code will further your knowledge on the consequences of drugs, alcohol, bullying, lack of sleep to name a few of the effects on the brain.

# Adversity

Many missing and suicidal teenagers and young people have been forced to play a dealt hand of adversity in their lives due to:
Poverty
Or abuse at home
Or by neglect at home
Or by abuse at school
Or by abuse within religion
Or by abuse from their peers
Or by trauma in their lives
Or by being in an abusive care home
Or by being lead-a-stray
Or by manipulative friends
Or by ...
Or indeed by all of the above.

Acknowledge what has happened to you in your childhood, move forward and build resilience to free yourself from your adversity. Please take the time to complete the ACE survey online and use that knowledge to make those changes that you need. I would also strongly advise you that the questions are very personal and could open old wounds. It is therefore better if you can make arrangements for a friend or relative to do this with you. I have also provided contact help numbers if you need to seek help or someone to talk about your traumatic childhood issues.

# Suicide Prevention Resources

## https://www.DontJump.ie

**Don't jump into suicide, find someone to talk to.**

**If you are that someone then LISTEN.**

If you know someone who has suicidal thoughts, give them a call and let them know that you are here for them and that they can talk to you at any time of the day or night.

https://www.mind.org.uk/information-support/helping-someone-else/supporting-someone-who-feels-suicidal/talking-about-suicidal-feelings/#.XX1fYflKjIU

# From
# MissingPeople.org.uk

**Scan the QR code to be taken to the Missing People website.**

If we all take a few moments to view photos of the missing, then perhaps you could find a missing person on your travels. The missing need all the help they can get.

# MissingInParis.com

Scan the QR code below, this will take you to the Missing in Paris website. Here you will be able to do the online ACE survey and it will host webpages from missing people from around the world. So if you are in holiday in USA, Spain, France, Holland, etc., check the website out, look at some of the missing photographs. And you might just help find someone and save a life. All it takes is two minutes of your time. Please do your bit. **Please Help Find Me.**

# USA

Of the **1 in 7** endangered runaways reported to NCMEC in 2017 who were likely sex trafficking victims, **88%** were in the care of social services or foster care when they went missing.

**Extract from childrenssociety.org.uk**

Key points: Children in care are three times more likely to go missing than those that live at home,

There is a clear link between going missing from care and sexual and criminal exploitation – the APPG for Runaway Missing Children and Adults heard evidence of criminal networks specifically targeting children's homes to groom children and young people known to be vulnerable for exploitation.

# Good NEWS from the Newspapers

**An Irish Teenager** family are appealing for information to help locate the 19-year-old who has been missing in Paris since Tuesday morning. He has been missing from his hotel since Tuesday morning. He had been in France for the Republic of Ireland's Euro 2016 game against Sweden in the Stade de France the night before, and was staying with family at the Ibis Paris Montmartre hotel. The Irish Embassy in Paris is providing consular assistance to the Donegal man's family. Meanwhile, the Football Association of Ireland has shared the family's appeal with its tens of thousands of social media followers. Anyone with information is asked to contact the Irish Embassy in Paris on their 24-7 service number which is 0033-1-44176780 or on twitter @IrlEmbParis.

**An American teenager** who was reported missing in Paris has been found, according to his family. American and European authorities spent Monday scrambling to locate a Miami-area teenager who travelled with his family to Paris, left a goodbye note and then disappeared, a federal law enforcement official told ABC News on Monday evening

Missing girl, 14, found safe and well. A 14-year-old girl who has been missing from her home for over a week has been found "safe and well" by police, Scotland Yard said. The teenager, from the Mansfield area of Notts, was found by police officers on routine patrol in the London Bridge area of the capital, police added. The girl was in the company of a 38-year-old man, who was arrested on suspicion of abduction and is currently in custody at a south-east London police station. The man awaits collection by Mansfield police. The 14-year-old girl, who cannot be named for legal reasons, was due to be reunited with her family.

June 2017 two teenage boys have been rescued, and are being treated for hypothermia, after spending three days lost in the catacombs beneath Paris. A spokesman for the Paris fire service said tracker dogs had helped them find the boys, aged 16 and 17, during a four-hour rescue effort. The catacombs are a network of burial chambers that stretch some 250km (150 miles) beneath the French capital. Only a small section of the catacombs is open to the public.

# Support Contact details in France

## Support from other agencies and organisations

| Organisation | Telephone | Website |
|---|---|---|
| French Ministry of Health: Psychiatric hospitals | | http://www.hopital.fr/Hopitaux/Espace-Sante-mentale |
| Find a doctor (GPs, psychiatrists and others) | | http://ameli-direct.ameli.fr/ |
| NHS | | http://www.nhs.uk/NHSEngland/Healthcareabroad/countryguide/Pages/healthcareinFrance.aspx |
| Association France Alzheimer Dordogne | 09 64 21 40 86 | Alzheimer.dordogne@orange.fr |
| MIND | 00 44 300 123 339 | www.mind.org.uk |
| Elisabeth Finn Care | 04 68 23 43 79 | Mary.hughes@elizabethfinn.org.uk |
| British Charitable Fund | 01 47 59 07 69 | britishcharitablefund@orange.fr |

## Do you have a website?

If you do, consider replacing your webpage 404's with a missing poster. Scan QR code below and this will explain how you can do this.

Or you could display a poster directly on your website or provide a link to the missing people website. You could even have a Video screen or billboard in your town square displaying information on the missing. Sides of buses could carry missing photographs, milk cartons, football shirts, street lamp post banners, on the side of trucks. Where else do you think? One thing I'm 100% sure of, **if it was your child then you would want their details plastered everywhere.**

# Madeleine McCann

Regardless of how long a child has been missing, there is still hope and as such we must all still remember to look.

## THE LIGHT FOR MADELEINE
### For Madeleine and the other Missing Children By Dave Smith

The candle of light Shines Bright
Throughout the Night
During the day, it burns away
A reminder for all to pray

We light a candle for Madeleine
Fond Memories reminisced
We light a candle on Madeleine's 16th Birthday
We light a candle to help us find Madeleine
We light a candle for those stolen away
We light a candle for friends and family
We light a candle for those still missing

Each Living day
Until eternity we will light a candle until
Madeleine finds her way back home

Light a candle for Madeleine and the missing
For we believe in HOPE and that the light
Will shine a pathway for families to reunite

Here is the official Madeleine McCann missing poster. © belongs to Teri Blythe. While it has been 13 years since Madeleine went missing, hope is vital to bringing her home. Please take the time to view photographs of the missing and actively look for them on your journey.

# Resilience

I would like to introduce you to my two concepts of resilience, functional resilience and dysfunctional resilience.

Throughout this book I have mentioned the word 'resilience.' Resilience is comparable to your backbone, resilience will maintain the stability of your being and will help reduce the impact of adversities that come along your way in life.

For those that have had adversity inflicted on them as children and then into adulthood. And for adults that has recently been subjected to adversity. Resilience will be your saviour.

Despite, the many thousands of self-help books, counselling services, psychological assessments people still suffer from their life traumas. CBT (Cognitive Behaviour Therapy) was hailed by health services as a quick way to heal people suffering from some types of trauma. NLP (Neurolinguistics Programming) is another method that can help people become resilient. In fact there are several therapies that help a victim recover.

However, the words "self-help" give the true meaning of recovery a personal meaning. In a nutshell, without your cooperation and full willingness to heal you will continue to suffer. Healing starts from and by YOU. You have heard of the saying, "to love, you must first love yourself." It is the same principal that applies in cases of trauma and adversity. Your love for yourself and your willingness for self-help will be two major factors that will help you build resilience. This in return will assist you with healing your past and creating a better future.

**Your stages of recovery**

No one understands better than you what adversity and trauma you have had to endure. No one can really comprehend what you have been forced to live through. And no one has or had any right to inflict adversity upon you.

I suggest that you do further research as this book is only a stepping stone for your recovery, more like an awareness insight to release the power within yourself.

Judith L. Herman MD wrote, *"Recovery therefore is based upon empowerment of the survivor and the creation of new connections. Recovery can take place only within the context of relationships; it cannot occur in isolation."*

The three stages of Psychological Trauma recovery:
1. Establish your own safety
2. Re-tell your traumatised story
3. Reconnect with others

My other stages of recovery from adversity and trauma are:

    A.) HOPE, retain hope at all times.
    B.) Understand your adversity and trauma.

C.) Learn to love yourself.

D.) Understand the importance of your own self-help. This is vital for a more solid recovery.

E.) Accept responsibility for your own recovery. You are not to blame. It was not your fault.

F.) Understand that religious beliefs are only that, a belief. Religion has a knack of making you a sinner and that perceived sin can affect your mental health. You need to rise above this and understand that no matter what occurred in your life, it was not your fault. You are a free person, who deserves pure equality with every other person.

The above are core positive resilience techniques that you need to develop.

Scan the QR code below to read a pdf by youngminds.org on Adversity and Trauma. It is designed for health workers on the frontline, but it will help you to. Take back the authority and power in your life, research and become aware.

**Closed mouths, keep it in the family**

Many people do not talk about the adversity that they suffered as a child, they hold their problems deep within their soul. For some they believed that they deserved this trauma which was inflicted on them as a child. As a child and as an adult they justify those beatings, sexual assault or emotional abuse as being a punishment for not being good enough.

In the past and even in some countries today, when a marriage or relationship breaks down the woman or man is afraid to leave or to speak up and seek help. The person in trauma takes all the blame, society and religion have engrained that shame as part of the marriage package, and the victim does not want to let others witness what they have endured for fear that they will yet again be punished or condemned.

You have possibly heard many stories about children who were abused by adults in their homes, schools, places of worship, in friends and other relations homes. Levels of the severity of abuse will vary quite dramatically. From a simple negative sentence such as, "you are no good at anything," to all three main areas of abuse (physical, emotional and sexual).

Negative and deeming talk to a child or a teenager is abusive, it disintegrates the capability of that person and they begin to believe that they are useless or indeed there is something not quite right about them.

In all of the above it is clear to see that the victim of adversity and trauma is not only fearful of the perpetrator but also from society and what people will think about them. The victim does not want, nor can go through the pain of other people turning away from them. But thankfully today we have many celebrities speaking up about the trauma that they have endured. By talking and speaking out you set yourself free. That is what you call effective or positive resilience.

**Nothing was your fault**

Resilience lets you understand that nothing was your fault, resilience turns the table and puts the blame firmly on the shoulders of the abuser. Resilience allows you to grow and allows your body and mind to heal. Resilience allows you to become a better person for yourself.

**Dysfunctional Resilience techniques.**

Trauma and abuse does not just happen when you are young, mature adults can be emotionally, physically or sexually abused, so much so that they remain in abusive relationships, sometimes by force or emotional blackmail. And when they do have the courage to break free, that adversity stays with them on their life's journey, it becomes their nightmare shadow.

As a result mature adults and teenagers sometimes turn to drink or drugs to free them from their adversity, these negative traits become their dysfunctional resilience. It is these negative dependencies that they begin to rely on. They numb the pain or so you believe.

But in reality drugs and alcohol make your life shorter and your problems longer lasting. These dysfunctional resilience techniques only help you in the immediate short term by numbing your pain in the "now." Such resilience does not help your past and it makes your future even bleaker.

**Your problems are sorted**

Wow, that's your problems all sorted now, right? I wish it was that easy, you wish it was that easy. Your thinking here is another self-help or counsellor telling me what to do, right?

Wrong, it's not easy, it's fucking painful and hard, and it's a pathway full of wrong turns and mishaps and thoughts of uncertainly that preys on your mind. These thoughts throw you curve balls that fuck you right up and drag you back to the gutter, and this becomes your perpetual routine of dependence on dysfunctional resilience. It is easier to turn to alcohol, or do some drugs, or shut others out, than face your demons, right?

The following story I'm about to tell you is completely minor to what you have went or are going through. But I want to make you aware that if something so small can make you do old routines again, then people suffering with adversity and trauma can be bombarded by mental requests to turn to dysfunctional resilience in order to dumb out their pain.

*"I stopped drinking tea and coffee cold turkey over two years ago. Before I stopped I drank around 10 to 14 cups of coffee*

*plus around 6 cups of tea per day. The first week of going cold turkey made me endure physical pain, I could not sleep or lay down, and my bones were in agony. But I kept going, I thought to myself if that much coffee and tea was causing me so much pain, then I don't need it and I'm going keep going. The second week the pain ceased as quickly as it arrived. After about six months I allowed myself a treat of one coffee per month. After I stopped drinking so much coffee and tea my health improved quite radically. However when Covid-19 reared its ugly head I started having one or more coffees per day. This became my morning ritual of going out to get shopping or going to work. I would stop at the garage and get a coffee and bun, sit in the car and watch the "new normal" world pass by. That became my comfort, my escapism from a world changed by a virus. Trapped in quarantine I felt the need to return to my old habit, certainly not in a way as before"*

The point I'm trying to make is while my problem above was not anywhere near the severity of adversity and trauma that other children and adults have to endure in their life's. However, the same outcome occurs, we tend to turn towards our old bad habits, regardless of what they might be. For example excessive eating, harming ourselves, hurting others, alcohol, drugs or whatever your dysfunctional resilience might be.

Now while my habit was certainly not anywhere near as traumatic as what your addictions are...the point is you do need to take stock and remind yourself that when things get bad within your thoughts and fears you must remember to practice positive resilience techniques.

For me my return to drinking coffee was short lived and it was not life threatening. However, when you turn to your old addictions they do become life threatening, they do reduce your life's journey on earth, they do trap you in a cell within your mind, and they do make you feel less of a person. The great news is, by adopting positive resilience techniques you have the ability to shrug it all off and weather storms that might have brought you to your knees in the past.

The power of your saviour is within your own hands, but you should also seek positive supporting people and organisations to help you along your journey to healing yourself and having the ability to stay safe. You deserve a health and rewarding life. [Each night you go to sleep, each morning you wake up, please repeat this sentence, "remind yourself each and every day that you are worthwhile and you are special."]

Some people believe in the power of a god, faith or religion to heal or help them through their adversity. But I believe that your healing must start from inside yourself and by yourself first. By learning to love yourself and believing in yourself, and trusting that you were not in any way to blame for what happened to you within your trauma or adversity, you will free your mind and provide yourself with the power to love and respect others. Become your own God, Pray to and for yourself, for your own recovery.

## Seeking Mental Health help

The NHS and ITV websites have a list of organisations offering mental health assistance, as such I have provided QR images that you can scan and visit for more information.

NHS

ITV

For some people their adversity has been so traumatic that it has made their life a living hell. This is so...so...sad that people inflict such torture and misery on another human being. For some that do these terrible deeds they too were abused as a child, they are doing to you what was done to them. Moreover, this does not give the abuser any right of lenience, but what it does provide you with is an understanding of why they might have done what they did. But please remember while this might give you an insight into their actions, it still does not give anyone the right to do what they did to you, none whatsoever.

## Relationships

Relationship problems can be talked about with two questions. "Why do you do it?" and "Why do you put up with it?" While these two questions inevitably require an open and trusting conversation between both partners, sometimes the person being abusive is unaware what they may be doing, so they could be in denial or believe that they are right in what they do.

However, if you can answer those two questions honestly then you will be in a position to decide the best course of action. The relationship might be so volatile that such questions if asked would put you in danger. Either way, the best situation is to be away from the abuse and then talk about it while under the safety of a third party. You're emotional and physical safety should always come first.

At no time should you ever accept emotional, physical or sexual abuse, you do not deserve it, and the person committing the abuse has or had no right to do so in the first place. This applies regardless of your age, religion beliefs or skin colour. Please remember that children are under your protection, as such they look to adults for support and safety. It is your duty to protect the children in your care from physical, emotional or sexual abuse. No one should stand by and let a child be abused, seek help and inform the authorities.

By acknowledging that your adversity and trauma was not your fault it allows you to let go and free yourself from your internal blame. It was not your fault, full stop. This belief is another form of positive resilience for you.

So if a blame thought comes into your head, what form of positive resilience can you use to stop it in its tracks? Well, everything is easier said than done, that's what you need to remember first. It will take hard work to change your thought process and self-blaming routine.

### The Internal Table and the Top Seat

I would like to introduce you to my practice of changing negative thoughts.

Rainbow Warrior is a Greenpeace ship that sails the seas to give hope for our planet and to fight for awareness, and environmental justice. If it was not for activists like Greenpeace then our earth would have been a lot worse than what it is today. That battle for hope still continues despite the environment knowledge that our world leaders now have.

Try and become your own personal rainbow warrior, fight to save yourself from your adversity and trauma. Create your own rainbow, this will light up your life and help free you from adversity. Your rainbow gives you hope. Being your own rainbow warrior gives you the strength to find the root cause of your adversity and crush it. You are a victim, but your rainbow can make you a warrior of your own salvation.

I recommend that you try and practise your rainbow thought process, this can also apply to most other situations as well, practice, practice and practise until it becomes a learned brain muscle and thought process of your own self-help action.

CBT facilitates a person's learning and how they can modify their negative thinking patterns. Thus actively changing the way they feel about themselves. By accepting your negative feelings you can facilitate a change towards a healthier way of life and create your own positive self-awareness.

Ok, so we all get thoughts popping in and out of our heads, right? Some thoughts are health while some are negative and can bring you down to your knees. If you dwell on the negative thoughts your mood changes for the worse. Yet happy thoughts uplift you. So ask yourself. "Where would you rather be?"

So, a positive thought pops into your head, you smile and laugh then you move onto your next task. However, when a negative thought arrives in your mind, you become agitated, and you try hard to stop it. You then begin to justify that thought and give it a meaning of importance. You internalise and now you have given that negative thought a seat at your inner minds table of divinity. And it's not any old seat you have given that thought, it's the seat at the head of the table. That thought will now begin to convince and convert every other positive thought sitting at that table towards a negative point of view about you. That negative thought is your abuser, it is your adversity, and it is your trauma. Why would you want to allow that negative thought to sit at your table?

So how do you try and stop this negative thought? You don't stop it, let it enter your mind, it has come knocking on your door and it is not going to go away. And the more you try and ignore the thought or push it away, the harder it will knock. Soon you will be exhausted trying to keep that negative thought out, so the door bursts open and you are consumed by your trauma and adversity.

So what can you do? Let the thought enter immediately, let it make its statement and demands. But don't give this though a seat at your table, let it wander around. [Definition of not giving it a seat: I mean don't give it any worth, do not accept what it is saying, and do not push it away, nor do you hold your hand out and accept this thought. The negative thought is not your friend it is devious and it will try and trick you into giving it a seat.]

So you let it wander around while it looks for a way to trick you into getting that large and nice juicy seat, the one that's close to the brain cell that controls your emotions and how you feel about yourself *(That seat that sits in the right front part of your brain, above your eyeballs, this is your prefrontal cortex (PFC). This is the part of the brain which is responsible for your negative thoughts.)* Now try and visualise and say to this thought, hey look over there, do you see that water flowing from the waterfall? Do you see the rainbow, isn't it beautiful? Do wish you were a rainbow? *[You can replace the rainbow concept with another memory that has a good positive impact on yourself or something else that makes you feel good when you think about it]*

A few therapist's will ask you to shut these thoughts out, but I believe that by doing so you are giving such thoughts more meaning and a grander purpose. The important point is don't allow the negative thought to control you, don't allow the thought to sit down at your table. The American Academy of Neurology Journal stated, *"If you do a lot of negative thinking, you wire your brain to be good at producing negative thoughts"* Can you see the pattern the more you allow negative thoughts to rule over you, the more you will turn to dysfunctional resilience to try and make you feel better about yourself.

The more you focus your brain on negative thoughts the more seats at your inner table will become negative seats. However, regardless of how damaged you are, there is always one seat at your table that cannot be converted to a negative seat. However, that positive seat can become hidden and muffled when it tries to speak out for you. But you can win back every negative seat if you reclaim positive resilience into your life. For example some people claim that when they accepted god into their lives everything changed for them. However by doing so you are still becoming dependant on someone else. You must first believe in yourself to heal properly.

That one positive seat that can never be removed is YOU. Your inner self will always hold a positive seat at your table. Your negative thoughts can and will try to hide and eradicate that last positive seat, it will keep trying for ever to convert that last positive seat. It is impossible to get that last seat. This is the reason why you are bombarded with these negative thoughts, they want to get that last seat. Fight back with positive resilience and reclaim your life back.

Here is an example: You were sexually abused as a child. You are happily cooking a meal, your partner comes in and touches you on the arm, and suddenly out of the blue the door into your mind opens. In bursts a negative thought, without any warning and with a defiance of not knocking or asking if it can come into your mind. The negative thought try's immediate on its own accord to sit at the top seat of your internal table.

You: "Hey, look over there, see that beautiful waterfall?"

Thought, "Do you remember that time your "xx" touched you? It was you're fault."

You interrupt, "I hear what you are saying, but I do not accept that, look! It is the most beautiful waterfall I have ever seen, go closer and see for yourself."

While you are dealing with this thought carry on with what you are currently doing and remind yourself of other positive thoughts, i.e. reminding yourself how you enjoyed that last film you watched, or I can't wait to eat this beautiful meal I'm cooking. But don't hide from the negative thought, be aware that it is still there, but offer it no importance.

Negative Thought: "Well it was your fault."

You: "Your words are hurtful, but thankfully we don't share the same opinion, why don't you look at that rainbow falling on my waterfall, it is such a beautiful waterfall is it not?

Negative Thought: "You're worthless, you made him/her do it to you"

You: "Look, at the rainbow it stretches all the way from the top to the bottom of the waterfall. That rainbow is as beautiful as me. Negative thought you are ok to stay and wander around my mind. But while you were once a part of my life, we no longer share the same pathway or the need for our self-blame. I'm worthwhile, I'm beautiful, and I will be allowed to be me. The past or present does not define me but rather that beautiful rainbow that you can clearly see, demonstrates where my life is and will always be, that waterfall and rainbow is my future. Negative thought, you have the freewill to change and when you do change, you to shall enjoy the beauty of our future and then you will be welcome to sit at my internal table. Until then I will always remind you, what happened to us both is now in the past. And when you enter my mind that beautiful rainbow and waterfall will always be there to help me and to help you, we can both recover from our trauma together."

A positive inner voice protects you it provides you with resilience. Practice this positive resilience technique over and over with every negative thought. Sometimes there may be a que of negative thoughts at the door of your mind, and they are not practising social distancing either. They are pushing up hard against each other, all fighting to get to that top seat and control your emotions and actions. Each thought believes that it will be the one that brings you down to your misery and back into trauma and adversity.

It can be tiring fighting these negative thoughts, but the most important thing to remember is; you are not to fight these thoughts, nor are you giving them a purpose or a meaning. You are purely acknowledging that they have arrived and you are allowing them to travel through your mind but you are not allowing them to sit at your table. If you need to have a conversation, it should be short and along the lines that I have narrated above. **At no time do you answer the negative thoughts questions.** Negative thoughts can only sit at your table if you allow them to do so, you need to give them permission. By allowing these negative thoughts to control you, or by answering their question directly you are pushing that seat closer towards them.

You do not need negative thoughts to remind you what has happened to you, after all you were the one that endured that adversity. What you do need is resilience to build your confidence and self-esteem. And while you cannot change the past, neither will you allow it to try and define you to who you are not. Indeed you are a person worthy of love and respect.

Another form of resilience is discovering what the trigger was that caused that negative thought? As in the story above, was it when the partner touched her shoulder. Was it the thought that your partner was now home and your dinner might not be as good as you had wished for? Was it the manner in the way you were touched, did that remind you of the way you were touched when you were a child. *[Even an adult who was not abused as a child but subsequently was abused as an adult, trauma and adversity still affects you and could destroy your wellbeing and mental health. So please also remember when I speak about trauma and adversity it does not only apply to that of childhood traumas but also adversities and trauma as an adult.]* Was it a sudden smell that triggered you thought? If you can uncover what the trigger was, then try and associate that trigger towards a happy moment. Or get your rainbow and waterfall ready when you feel your trigger getting pulled and ready for action.

I want to plant a seed of thought: When you learned to ride a bike, or become a gymnast or cook for the first time or anything else. You did not wake up one morning and say "hey presto I can ride a bike." Well maybe you did? I know I didn't, it took me many days perhaps even weeks of trying and practising to get and keep my balance. Each attempt was full of sweat and annoyance but with a worthy bounty of freedom when it was mastered.

So likewise it will take lots of practice at following the above story to stop negative thoughts from sitting at your table. Don't give up, stay with the programme, adjust it to fit your own requirements, your waterfall could be your Harley Davison motorbike or the view from a cruise that you loved or a nature programme showing you that there is love all around us if we look close enough.

Also remember that your negative thought was born via trauma and adversity. That negative thought knows no better. Make it your passage in life to teach and show that negative thought how to be free to experience the life that it should have been given. That negative thought, was born via adversity or trauma. It should have been born as a happy moment in your life, instead someone or others have let you down badly and it was born as an evil negative thought.

Your negative thought does not want to be what it is, but rather it was born into what it is. That's all this negative thought knows or understands. If it had a choice it would have wanted birth as a positive thought, one that can join you on a pathway and journey of happiness in your life's rewarding journey.

They say at the end of every rainbow there is a pot of gold. When I was a young boy I believed that story and I soon found out that when you chase a rainbow you never get to the bottom to find that pot of gold. And even today I still believe that story to be true. And I believe the reason you cannot find that pot of gold, is because each one of us… is that pot of gold. And that pot of gold has no monetary value, its value is your humanity towards yourself and each other on this planet of ours. Regardless of what has occurred in your life, you are worthwhile, you are loved and while you cannot change the past you can learn to live in the now and make your future a brighter one.

Your journey in life is a special one, shit happens, and it's so unfair, but in order to live you must move on. Bringing your trauma and adversity into the public eye helps get changes and results. When you think of woman's rights in the past when woman were badly treated, in and out of marriages, no right to vote or work, and how religions made woman second to man. Activism and knowledge has brought many freedoms for woman and rightfully so, indeed there is still a long way to go. The same applies to many other situations, until freedom and equality is shared equally then activism must carry on.

In regards to your mental health, you must be a healing activist and start with yourself first. At no time can you allow any person, society or religion to make you feel less worthy than any other person. No person regardless of colour, creed or stance in society or beyond is any better than you. In the eyes of the universe we are all equal without a shadow of a doubt.

I have talked above about how you can change your negative thoughts and how you can make your brain rethink and adapt its self. A book to read which outlines how you can change your brain via neuroplasticity is *"You Are Not Your Brain, by Jeffrey Schwartz."*

## Definition of resilience and why it is important

Resilience is defined by many however I have chosen the following meaning from everydayhealth.com as:

*"Resilience is the ability to withstand adversity and bounce back from difficult life events. Being resilient does not mean that people don't experience stress, emotional upheaval, and suffering. ... Resilience is important because it gives people the strength needed to process and overcome hardship."*

So why is resilience so important?

It keeps you on your toes, even people who have recurring bouts of adversity in their life have built in resilience. However, sometimes that resilience is not enough and they turn to negative resilience. Some may argue with me that there is no such thing as negative resilience. However, I beg to disagree and for the following reason. Some people turn to drugs or alcohol or some other addictive behaviour in order to numb their pain. This is a form of resilience, in reality it is negative or dysfunctional resilience, because it helps remove the pain and the torture of the mind or at least until that dependence wears off then you are back to your negative thought process and the whole dysfunctional routine starts over again.

This is what I call negative resilience (addictions), for its only temporary and it puts you in a worse situation overall. It numbs your emotions and feelings. Now you have adversity, trauma and addictions, and that's a lethal cocktail that will surely fuck with your brain. It is also a concoction that will make negative thoughts your master.

If you are in that category not only are you fighting the demons in your head, but you are also having to fight the feelings and thoughts of addiction (which again are negative thoughts). All of these are fighting for that top seat in your internal table.

This is what makes recovery harder, this is what makes physiatrist's so interested in the human mind.

Here you have a negative thought being rescued by an alcohol beverage and a cocaine sniff or joint thrown in as a good measure. After all they make you feel better quicker. It's a bit like hitting a child, give the kid a good smack on the arse or back of the head and they soon shut up, right? It is certainly quicker than spending time and helping or educating your child towards a more healthy life. Sure, a good smack never did you any harm, right? That's another negative reinforced learned habit. *"It did do you no harm,"* yet it made you believe that hitting a defenceless child is the right thing to do, right? How in god's name can anyone believe that hitting someone especially a child is good for them? Well it does demonstrate the power of believe and how you can be groomed into believing almost anything. A child needs and expects you to be its protector and certainly not its beater or emotional abuser.

I remember playing in the street and my friend's dad came home drunk from work after he had spent all his wages. The next thing we witnessed was their TV coming crashing through their window and onto the street below. Both my friend and his mother were regularly abused. They were Catholics who believed in marriage at any cost. Confession allowed him to forgive his sins while maintaining his stance at the head of the family and the authority on punishments for disapproving of his behaviour on a weekly regular bases.

My friend's mother could not leave her home. Where could she go? In those days there was almost no place for women to turn to for help. She had to endure the shame while enduring a weekly ritual or abuse. The police hands were tied as it was recognised by religion and law to be a family matter.

I was brought up in a trusting and caring household however my adversities developed from being abused by a gang of older boys while I was on my way home from school. Then by teachers at secondary school. If you stepped out of line, or didn't do what you were told to do, etc., you were hit on the hands and wrists with a thick leather belt that your teacher had baked in an oven to make it even harder. Most times when I got "the belt," I was badly bruised or blood trickled from my hands. In those days sadly the law did not allow the police to intervene and as such they stayed away from family or school disputes, even when violence was used as means of control.

Now, in most modern countries this is not allowed and offenders are prosecuted. Sadly there are many countries were children and woman are still subjected to such torture. Which is allowed via their society or religious believes. But there are many who fight for freedom and equality, sadly this comes a lot later when many have suffered or died.

## Addictions

When your addiction becomes exactly that an addiction, you then don't need that negative thought to turn you to drink, drugs, self-harm etc. You do that freely because it becomes a type of unhealthy basic need, and for some it's like food or water, it becomes a necessity, it becomes a dysfunctional method of addiction resilience.

Moreover, you can still turn your life around for the better. Free your mind from these negative thoughts by building up your resilience techniques. When you are able to deny negative thoughts any right over your body and mind, then your addictions will become less needy. However, if your addictions are so severe then you must seek medical or psychological help.

### Some types of resilience:

**Writing** is a form that I enjoy. I feel the need to write when things get on top of me or I read about injustices to our climate or children being trafficked etc. I find that if I create a story or poem then my mind frees itself from those negative thoughts. Action, doing something about the problem is also my form of resilience.

As such I have developed a brand called Story Lyrics, it is a series of interactive books that encourages you to write poems, stories or songs via the medium of your favourite singer songwriter.

**Sports or exercising** offers physical and mental health resilience by keeping your body health while nourishing the mind with natural bodily created endorphins.

Sex is another form of exercise that can keep the mind and body healthy. However, religion has demanded authority over your right to sex and your sexual identity. It has put forward a minefield of rules and religious obligations that make the most natural of things dirty or nasty. If you think or believe like that then indeed you will be filled with negative thoughts on what you are doing or want to do, and that in turn can induce negative thoughts. Even if you do save yourself for marriage, there will come a time that you do have sex but only because you have to please your man as laid down by your religious book of worship. This too will have a negative effect on your thought process, no matter how much you may believe in your duty to your believed god. Then you have religion and some others who object if you are gay. In a nutshell, your sexuality is yours and nobody else's.

**Religion,** for some their faith is a form of resilience that keeps them from harm's way and becomes their saviour.

I have spoken with many people who have believed that they were saved from their adversity by their god.

But, what I believe on this matter is irrelevant, what matters to you is your belief and how well you can heal and live a good and healthy life. But I do think that if you can love and believe in yourself and create a beautiful rainbow and waterfall for yourself, then that can be your god.

**Family and Friends**, can be there for you, being your rock of resilience in some cases. But not always, some friends or family can be toxic as they try to make you adjust to what they want. You are not anyone's puppet. You need positive support from friends and family that will help you heal. And in many cases these family units may well have been what caused your trauma and adversity in the first place. If that's the case stay clear until you can all heal for the better.

**Join a club or do something new**, it could be exercise, dancing, running, cycling, book reading, bible class, the list is endless. Why not even try an evening course on a subject or hobby that you are interested in. Meeting new friends or talking with people that share the same interests as you can help you become resilient.

### Comedy/Humour

There is nothing like a good laugh to keep you healthy. I remember going to a comedy club and I sat at the front. Yep, I should have guessed what was about to happen. I was bald and he picked on me every now and then.

Everyone in the audience were laughing their heads off at my expense, not once did they consider my feelings. But that was ok, I was fully in tune with my baldness, it did not affect me and that's what comedians do, they pick on people or situations and even sometimes shout out controversial jokes. I laughed along with everyone else. In fact I had two standing jokes of my own that I would engage with the comedians. I would shout back 1. Grass doesn't grow on a busy street. And 2. It was the bed post that did it to me.

When I was 18 my hair was down to my shoulders. I lost my hair in my early twenties, and it was no big deal for me, I enjoyed being bald, less hair to wash or style. Until one day a person in my life convinced me to go and do something about it. Reluctantly I went to a hair transplant surgeon believing that I needed hair to be worthwhile.

While seeing the consultant, I had an epiphany, I realised that I was happy and content the way I was and I was not going to change for anyone. If a person cannot accept you the way you are then they don't deserve you. However, for that short time I had allowed another person to inflict their negative thoughts onto me and that created anxiety and lowered my self-esteem. I used my waterfall to fight those negative thoughts that caused me anxiety.

But here is the beauty of comedy for some it can make you laugh in a healthy way about your own misfortune. And I made it my priority to go to a comedy club a few days later with friends, making sure we all got a seat on the front row. Because I was comfortable to who I was and I needed a good laugh at my expense.

**Stress**, just thinking about stress can stress you out. Daily life for children and adults can be stressful. At school you are under pressure to complete homework's, be on time for school, dress appropriately and meet the social expediency of your friends. Being a child or teenager does produce stress, so adults please bear this in mind. Adults stress can stem from income, jobs, home, and children to name a few.

How you deal with stress will translate to how negative your negative thoughts will be. You may feel that you are a horrible parent because you don't have enough money to get your child the latest iPhone. And the child could feel peer pressure when they turn up to school with a "brick phone." It's a terrible situation to be in. No wonder so many people are having mental health issues. The phone example is amplified when it becomes matters of losing your job or partner etc. Our current monetary economic society plays the role of the largest stress builder since your ancestors were born to earth. In those days their stress was all natural, it was basically the fight-or-flight response.

Now in modern days, stress appears out of the hairclip that you use to tie your hair back or from choosing what type of dog food from the hundreds that you can choose from. Stress is forced upon us by marketing companies or business trying to sell us everything under the sun.

Even making it an emotional crime if you don't remember to purchase something for mother's day.

And their sales ploys manage to cancel out the many days that you did something good for your mother. The truth and reality, these special days are days that we can do without, the stress they produce is unrealistic and unneeded. I always respected my mother, I did not need a special day to honour her, In fact my mother used to say, businesses are using these days to make a profit from another person's misery. [Mother's day is used figuratively to represent the concept of all other special mentioned days were you are encouraged to spend money to prove your love.]

Again your resilience to thwart stress could be your rainbow. Or you could declutter that stress and refuse to take part in things out with your control. Sit down with your children and get them involved with your family budget. Get everyone to make a list of what they would like to buy or to do. Include savings for a rainy day, holidays, clothes food etc. When children or teenagers are involved they begin to see that it's not a money tree that you have in the garden and they start to make informed decisions about what they actually need and what they can reasonably afford.

For example, there were many times when we were out shopping and the children wanted this and that. So out of guilt and to remain stress free from not being a bad parent we bought these items. But then the stress of having less money and spoiling your child would take hold.

So one day we decided to increase their pocket money and informed the children, "Whatever you want to buy, you need to be able to buy with your own money." All was fine, after all they saw an increase in money. The next time we went shopping, "Can I get this, can I get that." Our reply, "of course you can, do you have enough pocket money left to buy it?" After a bit of thinking we got the reply "Nah, I don't really need that anyways!" The child now faced with their own budget, decided how they wanted to spend their money, they took responsibility for their own money management. Plus that immediately removed our stress from shopping and the stress of believing we were bad parents.

When stress gets the better of you and the resilience techniques don't seem to work, get help. Sometimes that help might be simply arrived at. For example you have money problems, list your income and expenditure and remove items that you really do not need.

Other times your stress maybe because of your relationship, again take stock, make a list. Talk about your concerns with your partner, don't make it a situation of "your wrong and I'm right or you're the one that needs to change and I'm not." It needs to be an open conversation where you can both communicate as equals. If you cannot resolve your difference then get professional help.

On relationships, you do need to realise that regardless of being married or in a non-married relationship with or without children. You are both separate individuals with your own needs. You don't both have to be joined and sealed at the hip for every decision, every like or dislike.

Understanding this can help lower your stress. A true union between couples (of any sexual partnership) is trusting each other and being there for each other. Why not get yourself a positive book on relationships that you can both read and share with each other. [I suggest you both pick a different book of your own choice, a book that perhaps gives you meaning or purpose and use both books in your resilience relationship time together.]

**COVID-19,** and sadly the world will be feeling the fallout of this global pandemic and lockdown for many years to come. This pandemic has affected people in many different psychological ways. Fear of catching this virus and dying, fear of passing it on to close family, fear of loss of job and income.

Another concern is that of post-lockdown anxiety. As countries begin to reduce the regulations to your lockdown, uncertainty and worry can start to consume you. Sending your children back to school, attending work, going shopping could add to your anxiety. Some signs that you have this would include, difficulty sleeping, sweating, stressed about the future, tired and irritable. You could also become uncertain and this could stop you from doing normal routines or from enhancing your life. You may find an unhealthy balance of obsessively washing your hands to a fear of someone close by coughing or sneezing.

You can have a level of control over anxiety, by understanding a bit more about it and why? For example in this era of Covid you anxiety could stem from trying to predict or forecast your future, this is a normal part of problem solving. But anxiety sets in when you believe you really do not know the solution or outcome.

By taking proper precautions and reminding yourself that you are in control of your own thoughts and actions could possibly help reduce your anxiety. While the news is filled with "dos and don'ts," you can begin to feel anxiety when you challenge yourself as in, "is it really safe to go outside now, or to meet friends etc." Being confined in a lockdown is one thing for you, but when that safety barrier is removed it is quite natural for anxiety and concerns to surface.

So first of all recognise your anxiety signs then research and do something personal and constructive to re-educate yourself on how you can make your future bright again.

There is no doubt that Covid-19 has been a nasty virus that has not only killed 364,409 as at 29$^{th}$ May 2020, but it has also damaged the world's economy. The majority of deaths have occurred around vulnerable groups of people but everyone still needs to exercise caution and effective precautions, like self-isolating when sick and washing hands.

This virus has closed schools, businesses and worldwide travel. It will and has begun to redefine how we may live in the future. Many people are afraid of close contact with others, they hear a cough and they hide in fear of catching this virus. In reality, more people have died through pollution related causes than Covid-19. But people are still fearful of this virus.

The lockdown has stopped human interaction in a far greater way than playing computer games. Children in particular need social human interaction for positive play and growth. However, I believe that this slowdown of a fast paced life has also benefited people. But for some it has inflicted a greater financial worry, despite some government's claims of financially assisting its population.

People's mental health could be obstructed in years to come as the aftermath of this pandemic continues to have an impact on people's lives via many unknown future changes to our way of life.

The world is in this pandemic together both emotionally and financially, if the world is a "just world" then it cannot and must not let people suffer as result of any outcome on exiting the lockdowns.

Remember to seek out help and practice your resilience techniques to get you through Covid-19.

**How can you possibly know what I'm going through and why do you think you can help?**

Sometimes when a person has endured adversity or trauma in their lives they believe that no one can help them. And perhaps their therapist doesn't really understand because they have not experienced the trauma that they went through. So how could they possibly help?

When George Floyd was murdered by an American police officer who kneeled on his neck. No one needs to have went through that trauma to come to the conclusion that what happened to George was cruel, vicious and unwarranted, especially by a person who was supposed to uphold the law and protect all citizens regardless of the colour of their skin are equal.

Neither do you have to personally experience racism to understand that it is morally wrong and unjust for skin colour to make any difference between people. The remedy to fix racism is well known but sadly action is slow in coming forward.

People turned to peaceful protests as their form of resilience to overcome this tragic event. However, there were some that took this opportunity to create even more unjust havoc. For example the looting and burning of shops is unnecessary and unjust. These opportunists did this under the pretence of furthering the cause to stop racism. This type of violence by a minority creates unrest and trauma for others.

Likewise with death bereavement, sexual or physical assault, war trauma, mental health issues, miscarriage, abortion and religious issues. Do the counsellors or therapists helping need to have first-hand knowledge? And does it help if they do have such experience?

Counselling and therapists recommended that you join a support group consisting of people who have experienced the same adversity as you. That way you can share and help each other through your trauma. This support group is another method of positive resilience.

While your therapist may not have endured first-hand experience of what you have endured, they can still support you through knowledge and research into what methods of therapy can help you best. They have been trained to support you through different types of tested and trusted therapy. They have assisted many others in a similar position to you. Seeking help can be another tool for your bag of resilience.

A therapist that has endured adversity like yours can further form a "connection bond," but this does not necessary imply that they will be a better therapist for you and indeed you may never know what adversity they have endured in their life's.

Freud believed that having adversity can make some people stronger, however no one really wants adversity in their lives. Therefore, the solution is to put measures in place to stop adversity from occurring in the first place. Becoming an activist is another form of resilience,

I call this the "activist resilience program." By doing something about your situation, making people aware of what has happened to you, getting society and laws changed to stop this from happening to other people in the future is a resilient technique. For example, people fighting for family justice has insured that family law has been changed to make domestic abuse a crime. The fact that you are married or in a relationship should not give any other person (woman or man) any power over you.

Fighting for awareness and justice can provide you with a massive boost towards your personal resilience. You were forced to endure adversity, but now you can help others from falling prey to adversity.

**God**

I need to make one point of imperative importance, never... ever say that God must have given you that adversity or trauma, because he has a plan for you. If you believe that, then you are being led astray by a childhood negative groomed response via an extremely unhealthy religious belief. No one and especially no righteous God would ever put anyone in danger. If they did then they would be an evil God worthy of no respect whatsoever.

Your adversity or trauma was inflicted onto you by a person or a group of people or by a society and not by any perceived God.

If you accept that God has send you this punishment, then you have accepted the guilt and the culpability for what has occurred to you. Some people can relate to this and it can also form a source of resilience for what has happened to them. However, this is dysfunctional resilience. Remember, it was not your fault and no one from any divinity has planned that adversity for you and if they did then they would be equal to a devil. If you are to heal then you cannot accept or tolerate any guilt from what has happened to you.

Others either individually or in a group will use their power of religion and God to create an unhealthy believe that could cause adversity to be inflicted upon you. Some examples. The belief that a woman is second to a man. By forcing women to cover their faces and bodies. Allowing child marriages. Making a man as head of a church and denying woman to having any equal right to do so similarly. Forcing a child boy or girl to have their genitals cut. By making the woman walk behind the man. Forcing the woman to have sex regardless of in a marriage or out of it. Beating a woman because she is not fulfilling her duties as a wife. And the best of all is believing that it is a MAN who is God.

**Accepting responsibility**, while others were responsible for what they did to you via emotional, physical, sexual abuse, stress, uncaring comments, actions, or a mixture of everything. **You are the one that has control over your own responses to all of your adversities.**

The severity of your adversity can define how you may be able to handle this situation. If the same adversity was given to 100 people, each person would respond in a different way depending on what level of resilience they had managed to gather in their lives.

You can't change the past nor can you change what has happened to you. But you can take responsibility for your own recovery. Taking this responsibility into your own hands removes the power that this evil adversity holds over you. Moreover, it provides you with the power to heal and recover, this becomes your resilience.

If a time machine existed, then currently we would all be stuck in the same year, month, day and second. For throughout this world an injustice is done to someone, somewhere every second of the day. How this will be remedied is by building respect, freedom and equality for every person on this planet. Everyone deserves to be free from emotional, physical and sexual abuse.

Wealth and poverty are other abuses not commonly spoken about. How can society allow people to gather excessive wealth while others are in dire poverty?

While the adversity thrown at you was not your fault, you can accept the responsibility for your responses to that adversity. By taking responsibility for your recovery you have announced that your abuser can go fuck themselves, for you are now in charge of your own destiny. What happened to you is not right or just, it's a crime against your very existence. But you must reclaim responsibly for your wellbeing, don't let your trauma or adversity control or ruin your life anymore. You can do it, become resilient to the core of your life.

Accepting responsibility for your own wellbeing is the hardest thing for you to do, but it is also the most rewarding and powerful piece of armoury that you can allocate to your tool bag of resilience.

And after all the hype of positive build ups from books, sermons, church, mass gathering of positivity or you have returned from your counselling sessions full of hope. There will always come a time when you are alone or your mind finds a quiet time and a negative thought slowly begins to weasel its way into your mind with its eye on that top seat at the table of your internal mind. But remember, there will also come a time when your waterfall and rainbow will be opening the door and inviting them in. By accepting your own responsibility for your healing you will also heal those negative thoughts and your life will become a manifestation of your goodness. What has happened to you will always be there, but you will now know and accept that you are worthwhile, you are loved and you can be yourself again.

Take care and I hope that your waterfall of resilience will produce the brightest rainbow you can ever imagine. Please, please always remember you deserve a lot more for yourself. There are many more resilient techniques, I have only touched the surface of resilience. You can research for other resilient concepts that will help you overcome your adversity and trauma.

## Three points to remember:

Resilience will help you become a stronger person. And if you only remember three things recall these:

1. When you change your thinking, your life changes.

Think about point one for a minute or two. This works both ways, negative and positive. If you THINK that you deserved a beating, then that CHANGES YOUR LIFE, but it changes it for the worse. However if you THINK, that you are a worthy person and deserves respect then that CHANGES YOUR LIFE for the better and it enhances your life. So by changing your thinking in a positive manner, you enhance your life.

2. Take responsibility for your own healing, research for resilience techniques that can help you.
3. Resilience is the backbone of your life.

Lots of love and I hope you enjoy your journey towards making your life more resilient.

Dave ☺

## Quotations of Resilience.
Create your own rainbow by colouring in the words.

*"It's your reaction to adversity, not adversity itself that determines how your life's story will develop."* **Dieter F. Uchtdorf**

*"We are not a product of what has happened to us in our past. We have the power of choice."* **Stephen Covey**

"While we cannot change the past, we can overcome adversity by becoming Resilient." Dave Smith

"Every morning we are born again. What we do today is what matters most." Buddha

"Resilience is knowing that you are the only one that has the power and the responsibility to pick yourself up." Mary Holloway

"Life is about dancing in the rain while the sun sings its music and the rainbows deliver hope" Mimi Novic

"Love yourself, you are a rainbow." Dave Smith

"Resilience isn't a single skill. It's a variety of skills and coping mechanisms. To bounce back from bumps in the road as well as failures, you should focus on emphasizing the positive." Jean Chatzky

## Quotations of Hope

"You may not always have a comfortable life and you will not always be able to solve all of the world's problems at once but don't ever underestimate the importance you can have because history has shown us that courage can be contagious and hope can take on a life of its own." **Michelle Obama**

"Hope is the thing with feathers that perches in the soul and sings the tune without the words and never stops at all." **Emily Dickinson**

"Hope is important because it can make the present moment less difficult to bear. If we believe that tomorrow will be better, we can bear a hardship today." **Thich Nhat Hanh**

"When you have lost hope, you have lost everything. And when you think all is lost, when all is dire and bleak, there is always hope." **Pittacus Lore**

"There was never a night or a problem that could defeat sunrise or hope." – **Bernard Williams**

"Hope is being able to see that there is light despite all of the darkness." **Desmond Tutu**

## Missing Persons Poem

We miss you

So very much

Your touch

Your smile

You're Voice

Hope is what we rejoice

Each and every night

We struggle and fight

Within our minds we despair

In the morning Hope is our alliance

Rebuilding our resilience

We miss you so much

We know that you are there somewhere

We hope that you are safe

Everything changed

When we lost you

But, we will never lose hope

And one day we will have you in our arms once more

Hope and resilience is our open door

## The authors Vision, Pillar and Three main causes

**Pillar:** That every person should live in true and pure equality, no discrimination, no borders, and every person is free from emotional or physical harm and abuse. A world where every person is equal to the core.

On your deathbed, wealth, fame and power will remain, you can't take it with you. But kindness and goodness towards your fellow humans will go with you in perpetuity and on your next journey within the universe. This will be your only judgement on departing earth.

**The three Causes, help for:**

1) Mental Health Issues
2) Missing, Abducted, Abused & Trafficked Children and Adults
3) Climate protection

**Some of my websites** (There are many other great solutions and websites already out there):

1) **Mental Health:**
   a. **DontJump.ie** currently developing as a tool to support and provide people contemplating suicide with another point of view towards gaining back their will to live.

b. **MissingInParis.com** developed as a result of a true story and grew into a plan of action towards assisting people with mental health issues and assistance with finding missing people. The book and website also reviews Adverse Childhood Experiences and how they have played a major role in your upbringing.

2) **Resilience:**

   a. **StoryLyrics.com** developed as one method towards building Resilience. The concept is to form resilience by helping you to alleviate stress, anxiety and mental health problems by writing your story from the lyrics of your favourite artist.

3) **Climate Justice**

   a. Story Lyrics also introduces the author's term "Climate Cancer 2020." We must all do what we can to halt climate change. By become a climate activist and fighting for Climate Justice.
   https://www.climatecancer.co.uk

## About the Author

Dave holds a degree in Business and Psychology and is actively involved within the three pillars of his books. He has a Diploma in Adverse Childhood Experiences, CBT and NLP and has been involved within many aspects of psychological research. He believes that while good counselling can help a person, there is no better person to help you, than YOU yourself. Easier said than done, but never sell yourself short. You are born with the capability to form resilience and you do have the power to heal yourself. And there are good and positive people out there that will assist you on that journey.

Dave currently works within Climate adaptation, Mitigation and sustainability. He has carried out research within the climate emergency domain over many years and has worked with sustainability within the hospitality industry. He is passionate about the seriousness of the climate emergency and asks that every person do their bit to halt Climate change. Dave has attended the Climate reality leadership training course by Al Gore.

Dave acknowledges that he is in the same conundrum as billions of other people in their personal efforts to try and halt climate change. As such he firmly believes that governments and Politician's must be the leaders and make changes that are suitable for our future generation, our children, and do it now. Governments need to halt fossil fuel production and Invest heavily in research and innovation towards sustainable transportation and energy. That technology is currently available, but needs to be rolled out urgently and on a massive scale.

Electric vehicles are available but the affordability cost of these is bleak for the majority of people. As such industry and governments need to be proactive and make these affordable for everyone. Massive innovation into research re advancing the electric sustainability of aircraft is needed urgently. People need to quickly adapt to a greener lifestyle. Changing the layout of cities to become 'smarter' with less dependence on transportation, and with a 100% switch to green sustainable energy, these are a few of the many ways ahead to a cleaner and brighter future for humanity.

Video on Smart Cities, it is a start. https://qrs.ly/cwbdum1

Mental Health is important for human growth, visit Dave's website missinginparis.com and do an adapted ACE (Adverse Childhood Experiences) survey.

Missing children and adults is held dearly to Dave's

heart. He is involved with researching and looking for missing people, this has dramatically changed his outlook in life. He has written a book called "Missing in Paris" it is about a searcher called Mario who attempts to find a missing teenager in Paris.

Dave continues to look for other missing people in all of his travels and he believes that everyone can do the same. Together we can all make a difference and reunite a lost one with their family and friends. Millions of eyes looking is better than a few.

The news is filled with reports of fake and doctored images of models to creative artists to singer's songs being auto-tuned. The author believes that your true nature and purity of being a person and artist has been removed and exchanged as a necessity of unnatural purity and an unhealthy need for perfection. And indeed this can also affect the mental health of a person.

Dave's writing has no "auto-tune" it flows the way it is written, therefore you may come across English that might not meet the requirements of "proper grammar." He does carry out basic checks with an editor, but usually after he and his editor reads the first printed book, they realises a few changes might be needed. But hey, no one is perfect, nor do we need to be perfect. He makes no apologies, the concept behind Dave's Story Lyrics brand is to get everyone writing, to free themselves from negative or inactive thoughts and replace them with positive steps that can enhance their own and others life's.

As such Dave encourages everyone to write regardless of their education or perceived correct use of grammar. Most books that have been released have been edited and re-edited and puffed up for glorification beyond the capabilities of one person to do. This is a barrier, don't let it be a barrier for you. JUST WRITE.

The need for perfection is a barrier to true and real creativity, too many artists hide behind a mirage of perfection to give them an identity that is fake.

You are perfect, you do not need the acclaim from others to prove that. You are perfect.

**So as Dave says:**

- **Do** look for missing people on your travels
- **Fight** to end adversity for children and adults
- **Get** Writing
- **Become** a Climate Activist
- **Help** reduce mental health issues
- **Put** Health before wealth
- **Believe** in yourself including your rainbow and waterfall
- **Campaign** for freedom and equality for everyone, we all bleed the same blood, we are all born to the same planet and we are all one. NO ONE is any better than you, inside and outside of this world.

## Donation and Assistance

If you like what you read and would like to provide support for the 3 causes.

1. Fighting for Climate Justice
2. Finding missing Children and Adults
3. Mental Health & Suicide Prevention Awareness

**Methods of support:**

1. Become a climate activist.
2. Help find missing people
3. Become aware of mental health issues and how you can help others.
4. You can also make a direct donation at: https://www.paypal.me/ClimateCancer

**All income received goes towards the three causes outlined in this book.**

https://www.ClimateCancer.co.uk

I hope that you will never be in a position of having a loved one declared missing.

For the sake of every missing child and adult please take a few minutes to look at some of the missing photographs. And when you are on your day to day travels or on holiday, actively look as you walk and maybe you will recognise one of the missing. The more eyes looking, the better chance we have of finding missing people.

Protest and lobby your government to halt trafficking of any type, and to put more money into stopping this disgusting multibillion dollar criminalised industry.

Thank you for taking the time to read my book and as the TV program said, *"This is Doctor Frasier Crane, wishing you all good mental health, goodbye."*

# Samaritans & Global Helplines

It's late, but we're waiting for your call. Whatever you're going through, a Samaritan will face it with you. We're here 24 hours a day, 365 days a year.

## In the UK Call 116 123 for free

## Global help details

A list of countries where you can get help for many personal issues.

https://checkpointorg.com/global/

Or Scan the QR code below

www.ingramcontent.com/pod-product-compliance
Lightning Source LLC
Chambersburg PA
CBHW021140080526
44588CB00008B/143